MAKING
A LIVING
in the
STOCK
MARKET

MAKING A LIVING
in the
STOCK MARKET

BOB ELDRIDGE

Lighthouse Publishing Group, Inc.
Seattle, Washington

Copyright © 1998 Robert Eldridge

Library of Congress Cataloging-in-Publication Data
Eldridge, Robert, 1944-
     Making a living in the stock market/Robert Eldridge.
         p.   cm.
     Includes index.
     ISBN 0-910019-99-1 (alk. paper)
     1. Stockbrokers--United States. 2. Stocks--United States. I. Title.
HG4621.E43   1998
332.63'22'068--dc21   98-37382
                                                        CIP

Source Code: MLSM98

Book Design by Judy Burkhalter
Dust Jacket by Scott McRae
Production by Brent Magarrell
Editing/Proofing by Laurie-Jo Jones

Published by Lighthouse Publishing Group, Inc.
14675 Interurban Avenue South
Seattle, WA 98168-4664
1-800-706-8657
206-901-3100 (fax)

Printed in the United States of America
10 9 8 7 6 5 4 3 2

To my sweet wife Barbara, my guide
and inspiration, and my two sons, Chris
and David who have been my biggest fans
as we have all traveled down the road to
Making A Living In The Stock Market.

Bob Eldridge

CONTENTS

SECTION III
RESOURCES

CHAPTER OUTLINES

CHAPTER 6

CHAPTER 7

CHAPTER 8

APPENDIX 1

APPENDIX 2

APPENDIX 3

FOREWORD

$\mathbb{B}$ob Eldridge was a student in one of my seminars and now has risen to be one of my key speakers and trainers. What has happened between that first meeting and the powerhouse he has become is important and the very best way to explain is to give no explanation at all but to have you read this book. You see, "By their fruits ye shall know them."

To really understand someone look at what they do, what they perform. Look at their results. Then, more importantly, look at what drives them, what is their passion. As I've watched Bob develop he has a certain passion for cash flow, but so much more pervasive throughout all he does is his passion to help others. That is the essence of this book.

It is such a pleasure to see some of my basic strategies in the stock market (for generating cash flow) take on new and dynamic dimensions. Bob Eldridge has added new insights and distilled them into a simple, easy to understand way of making money.

Making A Living In The Stock Market gives you the tools and techniques you need to generate cash flow and accumulate wealth. Filled with examples and easy-to-follow formulas, it will enable you to uncover the patterns and secrets of some of the most powerful cash flow techniques. You now have in your hands the knowledge and strategies that give you the potential to not only change lives, but to affect fortunes, family dynasties, retirements, and financial destinies.

Great books have always been an important part of my life. I grew up feeding my brain great ideas by reading books about success. *Making A Living In The Stock Market* is that kind of book. As you read *Making A Living In The Stock Market*, imagine yourself doing each of the steps outlined. Mentally put yourself in the frame of mind to make investments that will put you on the fast track to becoming financially independent.

Once you have positioned yourself mentally for financial success, then the proven strategies, formulas, and patterns, which are revealed in this book, will make it a reality. Don't settle for anything less.

Wade B Cook

Wade B. Cook
New York Times Business Best-Selling Author,
Wall Street Money Machine
Stock Market Miracles
Business Buy The Bible

PREFACE

As I travel around the country teaching various stock market trading classes, I am continually bombarded by questions such as "Bob, which of these strategies do you use most in your own personal accounts," and "Bob, how did you actually get started in the stock trading business?" "How much money did you have to get started with?" "How long did it take before you were actually able to support your family by trading in the market?" I am writing this book for two reasons: first, to answer these questions specifically, and second, to pass on to each of you those principles and trading strategies I used that enabled me to resign my position as an air traffic control specialist with the Federal Aviation Administration after only two months of trading in the stock market. I really hope you are able to catch the spirit of what this means. If, like me, you have spent most of your life as an employee, then you have probably had someone else directing much of your life for you. When to come to work, when to take a break, when to eat lunch and when to go home are some of the areas of your life over which you have exercised precious little control. Perhaps less directly felt, but certainly no less significant areas include: what kind of home you will provide for your family, what vacations you will take, what kind of clothes you will wear and (this was a big one for me) what schools your children will attend. Think about it for a moment. All of these decisions, as well as others I have not mentioned, are being made *for* you, not *by* you, due to the fact that someone else is paying your salary! While being an employee carries a certain amount of security with it, I found that I had to relinquish too much control in some of the more important areas of my life.

In order to understand that *you can do* what I have done, it is very important that you realize who I am. You must be able to relate to me as a person, not as an author (I've never written a book before), nor as someone who has special talents or abilities. I'm about as average and ordinary as anyone you've ever met.

For my entire adult life, until age 52, I was a working man. I spent eight hours per day going to a job where a supervisor told me what to do and when to do it. My life revolved around my career as an air traffic control specialist with the FAA! My working schedule, and to a lesser extent, my leisure schedule, was totally out of my control and in the hands of the local controller's union organization. My career advancement and subsequent financial situation was often in the hands of others who didn't even know me! This is how *most* of us manage our affairs. We relinquish control of many parts of our lives (including our time) in order to receive a paycheck and the perceived financial stability that comes along with it.

Have you ever stopped to consider just how much stability such arrangements really offer? With the downsizing of corporate America over the last several years, many *former* employees have come face to face with some pretty grim facts, not the least of which is that any job (including yours) could easily evaporate at the next staff meeting!

A more insidious employee challenge is that of settling for things in life because you cannot afford something better. This fact was driven home to me clearly one evening when I was discussing college with my eldest teenage son, David. We had been talking about which college he was going to attend and how the tuition was to be paid. Various schools were mentioned, some of which were out-of-state institutions with huge tuitions. Being a very gifted athlete, we considered several scholarships for which he might apply. If he applied for several, perhaps he might get at least one!

Suddenly it occurred to me that I was looking for a way to get someone else to pay for my son's education. "Wait a minute, Bob, that's your responsibility!" a voice whispered inside my head. "But I can't afford it!" I reasoned back with myself. "I need the help that the scholarship will provide!" If the income provided by my job was not sufficient to pay the tuition for my son's education, then isn't it okay to seek financial aid? I suppose it is in some cases, but I really felt that it was my job to pay my son's college costs and yet, I was about to rationalize abdicating those responsibilities to someone else.

This began a line of thinking that changed my entire life! The underlying principle is one I'm sure you've heard before: "If it is to be, it's up to me!" I wasn't sure how I was going to accomplish it, but I was determined to regain my freedom, both financial and emotional. I was going to find a way that would enable me to provide for my family all of the things they needed, and many of the things they wanted. In short, I was going to find a way to truly be in charge of *all* aspects of my life.

It's easy to get excited about some things, particularly in the abstract, but it can be a challenge to actually put them into practice. As I began my quest to make some of these changes, I was confronted with *how* to go about it. How do people afford to live in large comfortable homes? How do people afford to send their children to the more expensive schools? Upon further reflection, I noticed that most of the upper class, if you will, were self-employed. The rest of us simply go to work for someone else, trading *most* of our time for *some* of their money! So maybe that was the key, to work for yourself, not for someone else. If this were true, it meant that before I could become financially independent, I would first have to become *unemployed*! Now that was a sobering thought!!

The successfully self-employed have a completely different mindset from the rest of us. Most are self-starters, requiring little direct supervision. Most have clear, well-defined goals and a precisely mapped business plan with which to achieve these goals. Imagine how many mental and emotional changes have to take place for an employee to become self-employed! Nevertheless, I was determined to change, so I set out to find a business with which I would feel comfortable...

After several false starts, I decided to investigate the stock market. I attended several classes on techniques and strategies and was amazed at what I learned! Much to my surprise, I found that making money in the market was not at all difficult, it was just... well, it was just different! I had to change my perspective in several areas. I learned to see the market in a completely different way. It was no longer the baffling business arena of an elite few. Now I saw the market as the "engine of the American economy" wherein *anyone* who applied himself could be successful! More importantly, I learned to see myself in a completely different way! No longer dependent upon my employer's guidance, I was free to map out my own plans for success. No longer subject to artificial limitations placed upon me by the FAA, I was free to become whatever I envisioned for myself and my family.

I worked very hard for two months, studying the strategies, making trades and trying to come up with ways to raise additional money to put into play. I changed to the evening shift so I could concentrate on trading during the market hours. I began trading "covered calls" and found myself making four to five times my FAA salary! At that point, I decided to quit my career of sixteen years and concentrate totally on the market as my new business! My wife, Barbara, and I had been married for 25 years and she had learned to trust my judgment, but this was a difficult decision for her. My coworkers were absolutely certain that I had lost my mind. My boss even called Barbara to plead with her to "please talk Bob out of this crazy idea!" To be sure, it was a difficult decision, but it has been the best business move I've ever made!

My family and I now live in our dream home, complete with a swimming pool and game room. My wife no longer has to spend long hours teaching school helping to supplement my salary. She is now able to volunteer some of her time to help at school and at church. We have taken several vacations we never would have contemplated before, and we are working on plans for an upcoming trip to Europe! I now can attend school and social activities with our boys. And by the way, we are no longer searching around for a scholarship for David. I am now able to send him to whatever school he wants to attend!

The purpose of this book is really quite simple. First, let me tell you what it is *not*. It is *not* designed to make you an expert in the stock market! I cannot tell you how to be something I am not! I do not use traditional investment strategies such as buying and holding stocks. There are many other sources such as stockbrokers and financial advisors to show you how to do this. Rather, I want to *tell* you how I was able to accomplish all of this in a really short period of time. Then I want to *show* you how you can do it, too. I want you to *understand* the strategies I have been able to use to generate huge amounts of cash flow, which I use to support my family. I want to *give* you a specific plan, which you can use to accomplish the same things for yourselves.

Please understand that this is *not* a get rich quick scheme! There is no "free" money out there and I'm not about to try to convince you otherwise. What I will share with you will require diligence and hard work! If you are not afraid to roll up your sleeves, if you are not afraid to set your creativity free, and if you are not afraid to follow someone who has already done it, then this will probably be one of the most important, life changing books you have ever read.

In order to make this information easy for you to understand and implement, I have divided the book into two sections. Section I includes Chapters 1 through 5 and deals with the basics of operating your own business. I felt this information was vital for those of you who, like me, have always been employees. Going into business for yourself can seem like (and is) an awesome task. There are some basic business principles as well as mindset changes which must be understood and mastered if you are to be successful.

Section II begins with Chapter 6 and covers the specific market strategies, which I use to generate an incredible cash flow. For those of you who are completely new to the market, I've included a chapter of very basic stock market information that can be found on page 137. You might want to start there. I want you to understand that I purposely *do not* cover all stock market strategies. While this book is designed to be only a starting point, it will help you to generate short term cash flow, learn to invest for the long-term and most importantly, return control of your time to you!

As you mature in these strategies, you will find that soon you will be ready to proceed beyond this level to other, more challenging ways to make money in the market. I can help you with additional material at that time. For now, however, let's confine our studies to some of the business and stock market basics which allow me, and soon you, to enjoy *Making A Living In The Stock Market*.

My hopes and prayers go with you.

OTHER TITLES BY
LIGHTHOUSE PUBLISHING GROUP, INC.

Bear Market Baloney, *Wade Cook*
Rolling Stocks, *Gregory Witt*
Sleeping Like A Baby, *John C. Hudelson*
Blueprints for Success, Volume I, *Various Authors*
Stock Market Miracles, *Wade Cook*
Wall Street Money Machine, *Wade Cook*

Brilliant Deductions, *Wade Cook*
The Secret Millionaire Guide To Nevada Corporations
John V. Childers, Jr.
Million Heirs, *John V. Childers, Jr.*
Wealth 101, *Wade Cook*

Cook's Book On Creative Real Estate, *Wade Cook*
How To Pick Up Foreclosures, *Wade Cook*
Real Estate Money Machine, *Wade Cook*
Real Estate For Real People, *Wade Cook*
101 Ways To Buy Real Estate Without Cash, *Wade Cook*

A+, *Wade Cook*
Business Buy The Bible, *Wade Cook*
Don't Set Goals (The Old Way), *Wade Cook*
Living In Color, *Renae Knapp*
Wade Cook's Power Quotes, *Wade Cook*
Y2K Gold Rush, *Wade Cook*

SECTION
I

BUSINESS

BASICS

CHAPTER 1

SETTING YOURSELF UP
TO "SACK SEED"

"Bob," my dad said, "Work hard, get a good education so you can get a good job and make a lot of money!" My dad was a great man. A product of the Great Depression, he learned early in his life to be frugal and never take risks unnecessarily. Raising his four sons, he never earned (or saved) a great deal of money, but we never went hungry. As an impressionable fourteen-year-old, I stood before my thirty-six year old father listening to these golden words of wisdom, absorbing everything, doubting nothing.

I took him at his word. Within two weeks, I had my first job as an usher at the only theater in our small East Texas hometown. Never having held a job before, I was very apprehensive, but I was determined to start early down that path to success. I wasn't sure what lay ahead, but if Dad said it, it had to be true. Over the next four years, I held many part-time jobs while in high school. By the time I was seventeen, I considered myself a workplace veteran well on my way to financial success. I didn't realize it at the time, but my understanding of success was exactly what my father's was, that is, a good job.

I finished high school and started on another leg of the journey, college. I just knew that this was to be the capstone of my plan for success. Living at home, I worked hard at several part-time jobs to pay my tuition, studying math and history. Vietnam came along and I served a stint in the U.S. Air Force. This was a really exciting time for me for at least two reasons. First, I loved flying and what better place to fly than with the U.S. Air Force! Second, I love this great country. So many great people before me had fought to preserve this free land with its bountiful opportunities and now I had the chance to add my name to that list!

While serving, I took correspondence and extension courses not wanting even war to slow down my progress. After my release from the military, I immediately returned to college and with the help of the GI bill and a part-time job in the physics lab, I worked to complete my Bachelor's Degree in math and history. I graduated in 1971 with decent grades; majors in math and history, a minor in physics, and a rose-colored view of the world. I had worked hard and now had set my sights on a good job, teaching high school math, which I found right away. Boy, was I excited! I had done all of the things my dad had said, and now was about to enjoy the fruits of my labor and his advice! Not only that, I had found the girl of my dreams and we were married immediately after graduation. Life was good!!

I was about to learn about two important financial facts of life. First, that schoolteachers don't make a lot of money and second, they earn every penny they are paid! My first year in the classroom, I earned $5,200. I spent as much time after class as I did in class grading papers and doing other teacher things, like attending school athletic and social functions. Since so much time was taken up by my career, I was unable to get a second job to supplement my income, so I finished that first year deeper in debt than I had ever been in my life! Fortunately my wife was now also teaching, otherwise who knows how desperate things might have become.

Most school districts have an interesting rule for their teachers. If they do not hold an advanced degree, they must complete so many hours of continuing education each year until they have completed at least a Master's Degree. In considering my situation, I reasoned that this must be a good thing because, after all, education is what guarantees success. Besides, when I finished my Master's, I would get a raise of at least $250 per year and maybe that would be what pulled me out of the financial quagmire in which I found myself. Keep in mind that at this time, the average salary was around $12,000 per year, so that $250 was equivalent to around 2% per year, or $1,000 in today's dollars. I was really excited about it! That being said, there was a bit of a problem. You see, I was working during the summer as an electrician's helper to supplement my income. Now in order to get that $250 per year raise, I was going to have to give up a summer job which paid me an extra $1,500 per summer! To add insult to injury, my Master's Degree was costing me about $700 per semester, almost three times what my raise would be! What's wrong with this picture? Let's see, I had a degree in math, so I ought to be able to figure this thing out!

Rules are rules, so I quit the extra job and returned to school during the next two summers to finish my next degree. We weren't extravagant, but the bills kept piling up. I rationalized that after graduation, I would have the extra financial steps on my contract plus credit for a Master's Degree, which meant that my salary should skyrocket to around $5,500 per year and with that extra money I should be able to catch up on the bills over the next couple of years!

By the time I had five years teaching experience, my wife and I had moved to Ft. Worth, Texas where I taught math at Burleson High School. This had been a good move. With the extra experience and a higher base salary in Texas, my salary climbed to around $9,200 per year and for the first time we were able to qualify to buy a nice little house. Understand that simply qualifying for a home did not mean that we could afford it. Things were still very tight. At this point, I had become accustomed to running out of money before we ran out of month. I assumed that this was the way we were supposed to live. I was so busy trying to stay alive financially, I failed to notice that I'd forgotten about Dad's plan for financial success! Isn't it strange how life can put so much pressure on us that we totally abandon our hopes and dreams and resign ourselves to settling for whatever we can get?! Let me jump ahead in time to make a couple of points.

As I mentioned earlier, I now teach workshops for students who want to learn how to use the stock market to generate income. To prepare these students for an intense two-day workshop experience, I offer them an inexpensive audio tape set that describes and preteaches the strategies that we will be working on during class. Then I teach them how they can work for themselves, making more money in less time. My first point is that I am amazed at how many of these students have experienced exactly what I did in chasing the American dream of financial independence! That is, the traditional equation of education plus job does not necessarily equal earning lots of money!

The second point I want to make is that, like I was, these students are really surprised at how easy these strategies were to implement and at how quickly they were able to get their attitudes back on track! After completing the home study course, their attention seems to automatically refocus on a plan for achieving their financial goals. When that happens, the day-to-day pressures of life, once so oppressive, seem to fade into the background. It's almost as if someone relights a fire long ago damped, rekindling those dreams and desires we all have in common. It is really incredible how very much alike we all are, despite our seeming differences in education, talents, abilities and socioeconomic levels.

My aviation background served me well. In 1976, I was offered (and accepted) a job with the FAA as an air traffic control specialist. My salary doubled immediately! I thought I had died and gone to heaven. I remembered what Dad had told me so many years ago. "Work hard, get a good education so you can get a good job so you can make a lot of money!"

At last, it was beginning to work. I was making more money than ever, almost $18,000 per year, and I had built-in salary increases for the rest of my life! I'm not sure exactly when it dawned on me, but at some point I realized that there was no college required to be an air traffic control specialist! You mean to say that I could have been making this kind of money without having to starve for six years attending school?! Now don't get me wrong, I wouldn't take money for my college education. But perhaps I had attained it for the wrong reasons. It was then that I realized that I and countless others had bought into a half truth. Working hard, getting a good education, getting a good job, and making a lot of money are all good things in and of themselves, but there is not a demonstrable cause-and-effect relationship between them. Education is absolutely no guarantee of making a lot of money. Not that there is anything wrong with educating yourself. That is always a good thing! But get the education for education's sake, not for any reason financial.

By the time I realized this, my family (we had two children by now) was fairly comfortable. We still lived from paycheck to paycheck, but we had everything we needed and some of the things we wanted. We were still in debt up to our ears, but then, who wasn't?! I had matured enough to realize that making a lot of money was probably not in the cards for me. But that was okay with us. Besides, "money can't buy happiness," and "the best things in life are free," and "a moment of love is worth more than a lifetime of riches," and so on and so on (I wonder if the people who came up with these gems were trying to rationalize their situations, too). So while we were happy, those little embers of wanting something better were still smoldering in the background.

Over the years, I would occasionally come across an opportunity to make extra money. Of course all of the multi-level marketing programs found their way into our living room. Their resulting products would also find their way into our garage where they became semi-permanent residents after the glow of the rallies and opportunity meetings faded. My hopes and desires would be briefly rekindled but reality would quickly return like a fire hose at full stream! So much for the glowing embers of hope.

Thus, reattached to reality, I would once again resign myself to letting my FAA supervisor tell me when to go to work, when to take a break, when to eat lunch, and when to go home. Indirectly, I was allowing someone else to dictate where I lived, what kind of car I drove, what kind of vacation I would take, and when I would take it. In other words, I was a typical American.

RECOGNIZING OPPORTUNITY

Several years ago, the Vietnamese Boat People began a huge immigration to the United States. This captured my interest because of my experiences during the Vietnam War. While in their country, I had admired their industry and perseverance under what were obviously trying times. So, I watched with great interest what they were able to do when allowed to take advantage of the opportunities available to them in America. I know that making generalizations can be very dangerous, but the achievements of this group of people appeared to me to be nothing short of amazing! When they arrived on our shores, they had nothing. Most of them had to abandon everything they owned in Vietnam and many of them tore their families asunder to make the trip. Sadly, many did not survive the trip and thus paid the supreme sacrifice as they tried to attain freedom and opportunity. The media followed them with great interest as they began to rebuild their lives in this country.

Slowly, amazing success stories began to appear in the press as this industrious and determined group worked to take advantage of the abundance they found here. Many became wealthy as they founded new companies and opened shops. Many more worked to take advantage of the educational opportunities. I marveled at the stories of young Vietnamese men and women who would work long hours at menial jobs while attending school full time. Not only were they prosperous at work, but also most were able to maintain almost perfect grades in the process! Recently I read of one such young man who graduated first in his class at West Point!! What a great people! What an inspired people! Or were they?

Could it be that they were neither great nor inspired, but rather just motivated? I believe they were just a people who had been without opportunity and freedom for so long that when they immigrated to America they were able to see the opportunities, which we as native Americans simply take for granted. Possibly we have lived so long with opportunity that we can no longer see it. Our lives of relative abundance may be blinding us to the blessings of the many opportunities which still exist in this country.

JOBS, A HISTORICAL PERSPECTIVE

Prior to the industrial revolution in this nation during the nineteenth century, ours was an agrarian society. That is, most people lived on farms, most of which were family subsistence farms. If you ate it, you either grew it or traded for it. Except for a few shops or small firms in the more populous areas, there were very few jobs to be had. Consequently, most people had to fend for themselves on small farms and ranches.

Early in the nineteenth century, many new technical marvels came upon the scene—the cotton gin, the steam engine, the sewing machine, and newer, faster ways of manufacturing. As these inventions were developed, manufacturing increased, creating an ever-increasing need for people to work at jobs, which previously didn't exist. Steamboats were now able to deliver, in record time, manufactured goods from the North to anxious customers in the South and West. Business boomed.

Back on the farm, generations of young people had watched their families work themselves into early graves from their never-ending, back-breaking daily routine. They greeted with open arms the opportunity to move to the cities to take jobs, which paid in a month what it previously took all year to acquire. Farm life was hard work. Today we tend to romanticize it with pastoral scenes—the crowing of roosters, the lowing of cattle, the smell of new mown hay and freshly baked bread, the simplicity of a time gone by. But make no mistake, farm life was hard, very hard.

As more and more jobs opened up, more and more young people abandoned the often harsh farm life for jobs in the cities. Slowly, the urban/rural balance was being reversed. People were willing to sacrifice the independence and self-reliance of the farm life for the easier and more profitable life style of having a job in the city. Suddenly, there were more people working for someone else than there were in business for themselves. This became the norm. Today, most people are taught at a young age that if they are to succeed, they must have a good job. In reality, the concept of an industrial America where most people are employees is indeed a relatively new phenomenon.

Those leaving the farm viewed the development of an industrialized America and the resulting societal shift from agrarian to urban as a blessing. By today's standards, most of these new jobs were difficult and unpleasant. But compared to what these former farm hands had left behind, they were attractive indeed! Working hours in the cities were shorter, leaving more leisure time. The salaries, nonexistent on the farm, allowed the new urbanite to afford to purchase those luxuries previously only dreamed of. What a life! Only 10 to 12 hours of work each day, usually not more than six days per week!

As families came to the cities and stayed there, a new mentality began to take shape. The rugged individualism, so characteristic of the rural American, began to give way to a more docile follower mentality. Over the years, parents began to teach their families that the sure road to success lay in preparing yourself to get a good job. To be sure, the independent spirit of the entrepreneur survived, but the emphasis shifted from farm life to starting new businesses. Of course, these businesses created new jobs and there were always people to fill the new positions. And the risks associated with starting these new businesses were tremendous! It took a stout heart to accept such risks when jobs were relatively plentiful.

RETIRING INTO POVERTY

Today, many of us finish school and rush right out to get a job. We spend most of our lives working for someone else and are content to retire at whatever our pension program will provide, perhaps hoping that Social Security will supplement our income so we don't have to depend upon our families for too much help. The underlying idea is that by the time we retire, our bills will have been paid off, we should own our home free and clear and our need for cash flow should be significantly reduced. That is the way most Americans plan their retirement.

Think about what I just said. We actually plan for lower levels of income, as if that were a desirable, or laudable goal!! A recent survey indicated that 80% of people retire at or below the poverty level. We actually look forward to these golden years without considering some of the financial facts of life. Consider just a few of them.

Assume that a person retires around age 65. Our children have already been raised and should be financially independent of us by this time, so our expenses should be going down. But now these children are probably married, with children of their own. That makes us grandparents, perhaps even great grandparents. Is it possible that our desire to provide gifts (Christmas, birthdays, et cetera) or other things like college tuition could, in fact, even raise our child related expenses? Is it possible that our medical expenses could be going up? Most elderly people are less physically able to do some of the home-related tasks, which were easy when they were younger. Consider mowing the lawn. Is it possible to spend $40 to $100 per month on a gardener or lawn service?

There are so many other areas like these where an elderly person's expenses will actually be increasing rather than decreasing! Many of us fail to take a hard, realistic look at what our living expenses are likely to be after retirement. As a result, we can no longer afford to keep up the house, so we move into an apartment, or worse, a retirement home. We can no longer afford to pay to maintain the car, so we have to sell it and have to depend upon others for transportation. Of course, we don't want to be a burden to others, so we stop going out.

All of this notwithstanding, there's really a much more important fact to consider. Our golden years should be some of the most wonderful years of our lives. We worked hard raising our children, providing for their needs, and now it should be our turn. We need to be able to afford to do those things we've always wanted to do, but never had the time or money to do. I've always wanted to be able to travel. There are so many wonderful places around the world to visit! If I had waited until retiring from the FAA, I would not have had the money to go to many of the places I've been able to.

CHANGING MY PERSPECTIVE

As I entered my fifteenth year with the FAA, I began to think seriously about what I had done with my life and where all of this was taking me. I knew that I wanted to make more money, but I didn't know how! Many of my friends and relatives had gone on to make small fortunes in businesses they owned and I felt as if I was capable of doing the same thing. But I had to work every day, and didn't have the time to spend opening a business on the side. Besides, I didn't know anything about running a business.

I began reading books on how to go into business for myself. Most of them were interesting, but they didn't tell me what I thought I needed to know. Then I read a book by Napoleon Hill entitled *Think and Grow Rich*. If you haven't read it, you should. Mr. Hill studied many very successful people to determine if there were any common denominators for success. He found two things, which really surprised him. First, successful people do share common characteristics. As a matter of fact, Mr. Hill found at least 16 of them! Second, and this is what gave me hope, all of these characteristics were learned. None of the people he studied were born with them! If they were able to learn to be successful, perhaps I could too. While I don't want to discuss the entire book, I think going over a couple of these characteristics is important.

One major characteristic necessary for success is that you must have a burning desire to succeed. You have to want it more than you want almost anything else in life! Up to the time I actually walked away from my career at the FAA, what do you suppose I wanted more than anything else? I would have to say security. You see, I was never willing to give up that steady paycheck in return for the increased opportunity of running my own business. Many years earlier, I had bought into the idea that true success was getting a good education so you could get a good job and make a lot of money. So you see, Mr. Hill was right. That is, my burning desire for security had brought me just that, security.

Another characteristic listed as being important was the ability to make decisions quickly. For most of us, making decisions quickly is very difficult to do. We have to learn how to develop this trait. I found that to be especially true in the stock market. Many of the opportunities, which come our way, will be available for mere minutes or hours at best. I have had to develop the ability to decide quickly to take advantage of these situations as they appear. As you begin to trade in the market, you will find yourself wanting to think about some of these opportunities. As I did, you will learn that this approach will wind up costing you more money than it will make you!

A final, very important topic to be considered here is that of surrounding yourself with a mastermind group. That is, start associating with people who are already successful at whatever you are trying to do. It only makes sense that if you want to be a great automobile mechanic, you should spend some time around great mechanics. For me, I wanted to be a great trader in the stock market, so I began associating with others who were already great traders. I attended classes and seminars given by those who had already achieved in the market what I was trying to do. I began reading books written by such great traders as Warren Buffett, Peter Lynch, and Wade Cook. As I immersed myself in their strategies, I began to understand what they were doing and I started to imitate them.

CHAPTER

FINDING A HORSE
TO RIDE

There are any number of ways to become financially independent in this country. What may work for one may not be suitable for another. Our challenge then is to find a vehicle which will take us from where we are to where we want to be. Let's consider a few of them.

THROUGH THE MULTI-LEVEL MAZE

A fellow controller once approached me with an opportunity to go into business for myself. "A business doing what?" I asked.

"Helping people achieve their dreams!" came the evasive answer. Well, I liked people and had nothing against helping them reach their goals, so I agreed to attend a meeting with him and his wife.

Throughout the meeting, I heard person after person stand to describe what a wonderful opportunity this was and how much it had changed their lives. "That's nice," I thought, wondering what it was that was so wonderful. After an hour and a half of listening to how people had built organizations and reached fantastic monthly incomes, a nicely dressed gentleman took the stand to teach us all how to build a sales network of friends, relatives, and co-workers.

Afterwards, all we had to do was to show these people how to recruit their friends, relatives, and co-workers. Product would flow downline to each of these people who would be out recruiting others and just look how the money would pour in!!

On the surface this sounded pretty good, so I decided to give it a try. Perhaps this was to be the opportunity I was looking for, and besides, it really sounded easy. I'd start by making a list of all of my friends, relatives, and co-workers...

Can I make a couple of observations here? First, one of the greatest motivators in life is dissatisfaction. To want something enough to make it happen, we have to be dissatisfied with what we have. A simple fact of life is that most people simply do not want to change their lives badly enough to make it happen! Second, most people do not have the level of determination required to overcome the obstacles life throws up before us. All of the great achievers in life had an unbelievable determination to succeed! Thomas Edison, Alexander Graham Bell, and Henry Ford all were determined to succeed no matter what it took! The potential for greatness lies within us all, but most lack the spirit of conviction and determination required to achieve that success. If you try to build a business based upon the motivation and desire of other people, you have to have the ability to make those people want something as badly as you want it. That is a rare talent indeed!

I was moderately successful at getting people to attend opportunity meetings. I was less effective at motivating them into action. As my sales organization grew, product would flow into my garage by the truckload, but it was hauled out only by the handfuls! I began spending more time at this part-time opportunity than I was spending at my full-time career!

I thought the problem was in the product. Perhaps people just didn't want it. So I changed to a different product. I began selling life insurance through a multi-level structure. A quick note here. If you are in a multi-level marketing program and you want to change products or company affiliations, don't plan to take your sales organization with you. It doesn't work! A few may follow you, but most will sense your dissatisfaction and will simply drop out of the loop! I learned that by experience. I had to work long hard hours to build an entirely different sales organization.

Again, I did moderately well. I had a group of around fifty sales people, but again, no one was selling. Everyone wanted to recruit and leave the sales work to the next person downline! I had incorrectly supposed that the problem lay in the product. Actually the problem was in my lack of understanding of what motivates others into action. The drive and desire must be internal to them! They must want success for themselves as much as I want it for myself.

After a couple of unsuccessful years of trying the multi-level route, I realized that this was probably not going to be the way for me. But this experience taught me a valuable lesson. It is necessary to try and okay to fail! You see, it was not until I had changed my perspective about how to make money that I was able to get started actually making it. I had to abandon, or at least reconsider, most of the half truths with which I had grown up. I had to come to fully realize that if others could do it then I could do it too! The challenge with multi-level systems is finding enough down-line people to make the system work and then keeping those people motivated.

That is the same challenge that everyone faces when trying to build a network. I didn't like having to depend upon others, and I still don't, so I had to find another horse to ride.

TRADITIONAL BUSINESSES

I have a younger brother who owns and operates a small carpet store in southern Louisiana. The challenges he has encountered have taught me a lot about running a business in the traditional sense. Here are a few of them...

First, there is the matter of capitalization. You need money to open a business, lots of it! You need a building. Inventory must be purchased.

Office equipment and supplies are next. Now you will need employees to help you, which opens up a whole new universe of challenges: payroll taxes, employee-management relations, employees who don't show up, employees who call in sick in order to get another day off, workmen's compensation issues, to name but a few. To pay for these things, you have two choices: spend money you already have, or go into debt. The vast majority of all new businesses fail within the first two years due to either being under capitalized or poorly managed. Most business consultants agree that you really need to have three to five years experience in a particular business before opening your doors and have in hand most of the money you need to start and run your business. A good rule of thumb is to have at least six months of operating capital in the bank after the other expenses have been paid for! That can be a sizable sum. My brother had around $300,000 tied up to open his carpet store.

Have you ever had difficulty finding someone to feed and water the pets while you take your family vacation? That's probably not much of a problem if your pet is a goldfish or a parakeet, but what if you have horses or cows? Well, if you have large animals and don't employ someone to watch over them, you are probably severely limited on vacation time. The same thing is true if you own a business. Who are you going to have oversee that business while you are out of town, the employees? The average business will last about two weeks if the "boss" doesn't come in!

The reason is understandable. To most employees, your business is just a job. To you it is everything! Your employees simply do not have the same motivation that you do in making that business successful. You have risked everything you own and they have risked nothing but time! Other than an occasional one or two days off, my brother hasn't had a vacation since he opened his store. In addition, he spends 12 hours a day, six days a week at the shop. For his trouble, he nets less money than if he had an average job working for a small-cap corporation. His situation is not unusual. Being a small business owner can have more risk than reward and the amount of time you have to spend each day keeping the doors open is incredible! I reasoned quickly that this was not the way for me to achieve financial independence.

FINDING A SELF-CENTERED BUSINESS

What I needed was a business that would be completely centered around me and my efforts. It must meet the following requirements:

1. **No employees**
2. **No customers**
3. **No overhead**
4. **No schedules**
5. **No liabilities**
6. **No sensitivity to the economy, and**
7. **No limits on income.**

For reasons I've already explained, I don't want the expense and hassle of dealing with employees. I don't want to have to please fussy customers like my brother does in his carpet shop. I don't want to have to pay fixed expenses associated with things like an office, utilities, advertising, et cetera. I don't want to have to report to work on a regular schedule. Of course I don't mind scheduling some working time, but I want to be able to work when I want to work, not when someone else thinks I should. I don't want someone, customer or employee to have the ability to sue me if they slip and fall, or spill a hot cup of coffee in their lap!

As far as the economy is concerned, I know that there will be fluctuations in economic conditions. There always have been, and there always will be. I simply don't want my business to rise and fall with it. I want a business that will do well in good times, as well as bad.

Most important of all of these requirements is income. I want to be able to make as much money as I need regardless of conditions which may exist. I want the potential for this income to be predicated upon my willingness and ability to work harder (or smarter) and not upon some arbitrary set of circumstances over which I have no control.

Wow, who wouldn't want those things? If we could find a business meeting all of those requirements, we could probably bottle it and become obscenely wealthy in a short time! In truth, there are a couple of businesses out there that meet most, or all of these requirements.

REAL ESTATE

One of them is real estate. Now I'm not talking about being a real estate agent or broker. That one won't meet even the first requirement, much less the rest! I'm talking about dealing with your own personal real estate property. Consider buying and selling (or renting) your own properties. Okay, we may be stretching requirements #2 and #6 a bit, but let's at least consider it.

Before launching my stock market career, I considered real estate very carefully. Do you remember back in the 80s when there were countless "Nothing Down" seminars promising overnight wealth, even if you had just declared bankruptcy? Well, I attended all of those that I could afford to. I learned a great deal in those classes. Most importantly, I learned that it is very difficult to buy many properties with nothing down. Yes, it can be done, but you have to really work hard to find them! However, I did learn a lot about real estate and even made a small amount of money on a couple of deals.

I came to love the idea that I was my own boss (at least in this part-time endeavor). Further, I found that I didn't have to do these deals in my hometown. I could actually travel to other cities and do deals there, too! In one such deal, I rented out my home in Louisiana when the FAA moved my family to Arkansas. It was a great income producer for the next three years. Then a strange thing happened...

All of a sudden the real estate market went south, way south! Rents started coming down to the point where they would no longer cover the mortgage payment! Keep in mind here that you don't control what you can rent a property for nearly as much as the market does! So much for requirement #6! Fortunately, I didn't get hurt too badly because I only owned a couple of properties, but I know many people who lost a lot of money. I sold my Louisiana house for a $30,000 loss and was happy it wasn't more! But isn't this the ideal time to buy real estate, when the market is down? Yes, but again you have to have either money or a huge line of credit to be able to capitalize on shifting real estate markets.

Don't misunderstand me, I know many people who make a lot of money in real estate. They believe it is one of the best businesses in the world. And I'm sure it is...for them! It does meet almost all of the requirements I set above. But there is something even better out there!

TAKING STOCK OF THE MARKET

With shifting economic conditions, my real estate career came slamming to an end! I once again resigned myself to finishing out my days working as an air traffic control specialist for the FAA. And, in reality, it was a great job! By 1995, my income had risen to around $70,000 per year. Please understand that I was not cash flowing $70,000 per year! That was the total value of my yearly compensation including benefits. I was cash flowing a little more than half of that! But life was good! My family and I lived in Jonesboro, Arkansas in a nice home located in a great neighborhood. I had even been able to scrape together enough extra money each month to own two airplanes! That sounds more impressive than it really was. I had built one of them, and the other was an old Beechcraft Bonanza. They were not "high dollar" aircraft, but I was able to afford to fly when I wanted to. Yes indeed, life was good.

Shortly after moving to Arkansas, I began to watch Wal-mart stock. I noticed that it usually traded around $19 and would occasionally run up to around $22 or $23 and then settle back to around $19. I decided that the next time Wal-mart got back down to $19, I would buy some of it and ride it back up. To be prepared, I opened an account with one of the major discount brokerage firms. A few weeks later, the stock settled back to $18 and I bought 100 shares and began to watch it every day. Within a month, Wal-mart was trading at $22, so I sold it. Wow! I had just made around $250 after commissions! Over the next few months, I repeated this two more times, thinking that I had found the only stock in the world which had this behavior!

I thought this had possibilities, so I attended a class to learn more about other ways to make money in the market. What I discovered was astounding! There are more ways to make money in the market than I had ever imagined. I picked a strategy which I understood (more or less) and went to work!

The strategy was covered calls. It was elegant in its simplicity! You buy a stock and then sell someone the right to buy it from you for a higher price than what you paid for it. They may or may not buy it from you, but in either case, they pay you for that right! I had $6,000 in my brokerage account, so I decided to try one. I bought 1,000 shares of a company called Copytele, Inc. at $12 per share. Notice that I only had $6,000 to spend, so I had to buy the stock on margin. This means you only have to put up half of the money. The broker will lend you the balance if the stock is marginable. I'll further discuss margin in Chapter 13. As soon as the broker confirmed that I had purchased the stock, I sold the $12.50 calls for the next month. That is, I sold someone the right to buy the stock from me at $12.50. For this, they paid me $1.50 per share. Let's see, $1.50 per share on 1,000 shares, that's $1,500! Did you understand what had just happened? I invested $6,000 of my cash and had received $1,500 for it! A $1,500 return on a $6,000 investment! That's a 25% return for the month!

During the rest of the class, I learned several other strategies, none of which I really understood. I did, however, understand what I had just done with covered calls! I returned home with the sure and certain knowledge that I had found the business that was going to set us free financially if we were willing to make some initial sacrifices! Over the next month, my family and I worked to raise as much capital as we could. We sold a beautiful 3,500 square foot home and moved into a 1,300 square foot rental house.

We sold this beautiful 3,500 square foot home

and moved into this 1,300 square foot rental house

I had worked hard to get to a point in my life where I could afford to do a lot of flying and I really valued the time I was able to spend aloft. However, in order to help raise more money with which to trade, we decided to sell one of my airplanes. We sold the homebuilt. You can never know how much of a sacrifice that really was unless you have built and flown one yourself. It was almost like selling one of my children!

I also sold this homebuilt aircraft to raise money

Finally, we rearranged existing financing on several other things in an effort to cut our monthly cost of living as much as we could. In all, we reduced our monthly expenses by over $1,500 and raised around $50,000 cash with which I began trading immediately! There was no doubt about which strategy to use. I began writing covered calls.

In his book, *Think and Grow Rich*, Napoleon Hill identified 16 different learned characteristics all successful people have in common. I described one of these characteristics as having a "burning desire" to accomplish something. As I look back over what I've been able to do in the stock market, I can see that I had such a desire! I was willing to sell one of my airplanes (a real sacrifice) and move my family from a 3,500 square foot home into a 1,300 square foot rental house. Knowing what I know now, I can assure you that this is exactly the attitude required to be successful in anything you want to do. If you approach any activity with half-hearted resolve, you will not have the strength to withstand the challenges with which you will inevitably be faced. One purpose of this book is to teach you specific methods and strategies that will enable you to retire (or resign) quickly. It can be done. I can teach you how. I can supply the strategies. However, you must supply the desire!

My first full month of selling covered calls, I cleared around $24,000. The second month, I netted around $20,000. During my first full year of covered call writing, I averaged a little over a 20% return each month! I attended the class in October and resigned from the FAA the next December—two months later! At long last, I had found the business I had been looking for. It met all of the requirements I had set. I had no customers, no employees, and no schedules. This was an opportunity that was dependent upon me and me alone for success. I didn't have to deal with deadlines, supervisors or income limitations. I was free to work when and where I wanted to and set my own hours and income level.

It was hard to leave the FAA after 16 years. You see I didn't just give up a job, I gave up my career, my identity! As I look back on it, there really wasn't much to decide. If I stayed, I could look forward to earning around $70,000 per year for the next four or five years then retiring with around $1,800 per month. By making the tough decision to go into business for myself, I increased my cash flow around ten fold during the first year alone! I made more my first year in the market than I would have with the FAA over the next five years! So what do you think, was that a hard decision? You bet it was! Other than getting married 27 years ago, it was the hardest decision I've ever made, but it has been the best financial move I have ever made!

What made that decision so hard was not wondering if the money was really going to be there when I needed it. The difficult part was not financial at all. It was personal. It was emotional. You see, I had been taught all of my life that the key to success was hard work and a good education, both of which led to a good job and lots of money. The difficulty here was overcoming years of learned misinformation. The tough part is trusting in the fact that if others could do this that I could too, that I was just as capable as anyone else if I was willing to exercise the faith in myself to do whatever it took to get the job done!

What would you have done, faced with the same circumstances? Better yet, what will you do when you are faced with the same circumstances?

CHAPTER

PLAN YOUR WORK AND THEN WORK YOUR PLAN

If you look carefully at the way most Americans live their lives, you will probably discern a pronounced case of "money management myopia." Many of us are simply not able to manage money beyond next week's paycheck. Not being able to afford to pay for things we want, we simply charge them. We have developed the very dangerous habit of granting ourselves plastic raises when we run short of cash. This fact is painfully evident in the rapidly rising number of personal bankruptcies.

There are many reasons for this, not the least of which is what I refer to as "fiscal illiteracy." People are simply never taught how money works. Nowhere in elementary school, high school or even in most undergraduate college programs are students ever taught what to do with their money once they enter their earning years! They are simply left to their own devices and more often than not find themselves blithely following the incorrect examples set by others.

As I described earlier in the book, much of my adult working life was devoted to managing money the way I saw others managing theirs.

Most of the examples I saw and followed were based upon the concept of "if you can't afford it, then charge it!" I was taught how to work for money, but I was never taught the importance of learning how to make your money work for you. If you are normal, you are probably working under the same handicaps, so let's take a moment to review a few of the money management principles, which are important to understand if you are to make this business work for you.

First, get good at distinguishing between your wants and your needs. When making financial decisions, particularly in deciding whether or not to make a purchase, develop the ability to remove the emotion from the decision. Avoid rationalizing! If you truly need something, then by all means, buy it! But be sure your reasoning is sound. For example, on too many occasions I've used the following line of thought to rationalize buying a new car. My old car really has a lot of miles on it. Cars with high miles tend to break down quite often and the repair bills can really be expensive. So let's buy a new car that will be more dependable, with fewer breakdowns and we'll probably save money on repair bills in the long run! Sound familiar? Did I really *need* a new car, or did I simply *want* one? The answer should be obvious. I wanted the new car, and I was going to think of every reason I could to justify spending that money! I loved the fresh paint, and oh, the sweet smell of a new interior! How about this one... I'm getting a really great deal! The sticker price is $25,000 and the dealer is giving me $5,000 off. The car will only cost me $20,000 and I can finance it over six years, so the payments will be really low! Not one of these statements is a demonstration of a need. Rather, they are justifications of a want. Think rationally about the true cost of that great deal. Over the next six years, you are going to be making payments on an asset, which is losing an average of over 12% per year. That means that at the end of the six-year period, your investment will have lost over 70% of its value! Now how great does that deal look?

Next, learn to recognize and control impulse buying. Whenever you want to make a purchase, never make the purchase the same day you start thinking about it. Following this simple rule will eliminate the vast majority of your impulse buys. And if you don't think you're prone to impulse buying, I want you to notice something the next time you go to the supermarket. When you get to the checkout stand, look closely at what's there. Do you see a rack with all kinds of little doo-dads for sale? In most stores, you'll find small things like key rings, batteries, magazines, pens, et cetera. It's those little last minute items, which have the highest markup percentage for the store. You probably don't think much about it because the price is so comparatively low. Retail marketing managers know these things and are trained to take advantage of them (or us). Impulse buying is why eye-level shelf space is so prized! If you see it, you will probably buy it.

Save 10% of everything you earn, without fail. I know you've heard that one before, but it's so important! Before going into the stock market as a business, my savings habits were as bad as my spending habits. After working (and spending) all my adult life, I only had around $6,000 cash that I could put my hands on. Some of you have probably done a lot better than I did, but very few, if any, of you have 10% of everything you've ever earned! Why do you suppose that is? In my view, we don't save money because we don't understand what to do with it once we have it. We don't realize how powerful that money could be if we knew how to really put it to work! Saving 10% of our income each year would give us the cash equivalent of a full year's salary in 10 years, not counting growth from interest. Just that money, if invested properly could easily triple or quadruple our retirement income! Develop the self-discipline required to begin a regular savings program now!

While these are not the only money management principles you should master, they are certainly some of the biggies. If you are going to be successful in making the stock market a business, you must learn how to manage your money responsibly. Remember, it's not how much money you make that's important, it's how much money you keep!

CREATING AN ASSET BASE

As with any business, you must begin with some assets. Most businesses fail at least partly because they are under capitalized. In order to be successful in making a living in the stock market or any other business, you have to have enough capital to enable you to "weather the storms." If you do not have an asset base, you sometimes have to get pretty resourceful in order to create one.

EXISTING CASH

To the maximum extent possible, try to use whatever cash you have lying around. Current savings accounts are a good place to start. If you have to start small, that's all right, but maximize your returns by maximizing the amount with which you start. When I began trading, I started part time because I only had $6,000. This was not enough of an asset base with which to begin supporting my family! At the time, I was an air traffic control specialist with the FAA, making around $70,000 per year. This income was the asset base I used to begin my trading career. I borrowed the money to attend a class on stock market trading strategies. I then used the income from my job to repay that loan, which was really charged to my Mastercard. At that class, I learned about the power and safety of covered calls and promptly put all of the $6,000 into one covered call play. This experience taught me a couple of things.

First, it taught me that covered calls are a good place to begin to learn about the market. The play is relatively safe and you will gain invaluable experience in dealing with options. Second, it taught me that returns of from twelve to twenty percent per month are reasonable to expect. My first play was a 25% return!

TURN STAGNANT ASSETS INTO CASH

Almost without exception, most of us have things lying around that can be turned into cash. We need to be astute enough to recognize them, creative enough to itemize them and courageous enough to utilize them. While my job with the FAA was supporting my family, it was not producing enough of an income to put much additional money into the market. I was alert enough to realize that if I were ever going to be able to make this a paying business, I was going to have to develop an asset base outside of what funds I could break free from my job. It was only then that I began to understand how badly I wanted this business to work for me. I began to realize that I did indeed have that *burning desire* described in *Think And Grow Rich*.

This desire to get my business off the ground led me and my family through some rather tough decisions. My family and I decided to sacrifice some things to raise the money we needed to get started. We lived in a beautiful, large home in a great part of town. We sold it! We bought and moved into a small rental house on the other side of town, putting most of the price difference into our trading account. I sold an airplane, which I had built. This gave us a little more cash with which to work. These were hard decisions and having the courage to act upon them was one of the things, which helped to solidify our commitment to making this business work for us.

DEBT LEVERAGING

If you cannot raise any money through either of the two methods above, there is another way. You can borrow it, but please exercise caution here! Staying out of debt is always a good idea and going into debt to finance highly speculative market trades can be disastrous! My years of experience have taught me that there are two types of debt—soft debt and hard debt.

Soft debt I'll define as any debt which is totally covered by an asset. For example, if you borrow money on the equity in your home, you have created soft debt because that debt can be eliminated by liquidating your home. Not a pleasant thought, perhaps, but the debt is totally covered by an asset, which can be sold to retire that debt.

Hard debt is debt which is not totally covered by an underlying asset. For example, revolving credit card debt is hard debt. The amount owed is not covered by an asset, which can be sold to retire the debt. Depending upon how they're financed, automobiles can be either hard or soft debt. Most people pay the minimum down and finance for the longest period possible. This is the hardest of hard debt because you instantly owe more on the car than it is worth. Unless you can come up with the difference in cash, you cannot sell the car for enough to totally pay it off.

When hard times come, it is hard debt, which can force families into bankruptcy. Selling something can eliminate soft debt. If you must go into debt, avoid hard debt! If you must borrow money to get your business started, arrange your affairs so that you use soft debt. Always have an escape plan! Never put yourself or more importantly, your family in the dangerous position of having to make a profit to stay above water! If you borrow $50,000 to get into the market, do so only using soft debt. That way, if you lose in the market, you will be able to repay what you owe by selling the underlying assets. A well-respected church leader once told me that failing to repay what you have borrowed is the same as stealing. By definition then, you should probably avoid unsecured loans to raise money for trading in the market.

The bottom line is that you are going to need to have some cash with which to trade. You can use existing cash, you can sell something, or you can borrow it. In my experience, you can expect to need around $50,000 to consistently generate enough cash to support your family. Anything less than that amount will probably put too much stress on you as you try to pull excessive, unrealistic profits from each deal. This situation can force you into panic management types of decisions.

If you have in excess of $50,000, you would probably be wise not to put all of it into high yield strategies. High yield can be a double-edged sword, the other edge being high risk! If you are fortunate enough to have a large asset base, in Chapter 11 you will learn a strategy which will probably be a more prudent route for you to take.

These principles are very important to understand and use in our everyday lives because if we are unable to manage our personal finances, we will fare little better in our businesses. Other than being undercapitalized, one of the most frequent reasons for small business failure is poor management. Poor business financial management techniques can be a direct result of poor personal financial management and both can have equally devastating consequences.

CHAPTER 4

STRUCTURING YOUR BUSINESS

For everyone's protection, I want to start this chapter with a disclaimer. I am not an attorney. I am not an accountant, certified or otherwise. I am not a financial planner. I am none of these things and I don't want to be. I pay professionals a lot of money to handle these matters for me.

What I discuss here, I do so from a layman's point of view. When I structured my business affairs, I had the help of others who are highly qualified in these fields. Before you decide how to structure yourself, you should seek the advice of competent professionals in the legal and tax fields. But be very careful in choosing those who will be guiding you. The typical accountant or lawyer will not be of much help to you. You should look for those who are willing and able to take your affairs to the next level through creative yet legal combinations of corporations, trusts, and other entities. Now that that's out of the way, let's get on with it!

PRIVATE OWNERSHIP VS. CORPORATIONS

When my brother opened his carpet shop in southern Louisiana, he did so as a sole proprietorship. In any business, this can be extremely hazardous to your fiscal health! Consider first what happens to your income.

In this arrangement, most income is treated as ordinary or "earned" income. This means it is subject to FICA, more commonly called Social Security taxes. When you are employed, you have these taxes (about 7 1/2%) withheld from your paycheck, but that's not the whole story. The really bad news is that your employer must pay an additional 7 1/2% for you. That's a total of around 15% taxation before you even start talking about federal income taxes. When you are self-employed in a sole proprietorship, you are the employee and you are the employer, so you foot the bill for the entire 15%!

As if this weren't bad enough, federal income taxes also have to be paid. All of his income is taxed to him at personal income tax rates, which can be as high as around 40%, depending on how well his business actually does. This means that if he has a really good year and earns around $100,000, his total federal tax liability could be as high as almost $55,000!! It is almost as if the various governmental bodies were trying to discourage industry and thrift, the very things which have helped to make this country so great!

An additional concern is liability. Any self-employed person using this system must assume all responsibility for his or her actions as well as those of any other employees. As prudent people, we can control our actions and, to a limited extent, our exposure to liability. However, we have much less control over the actions of our employees. A few years ago this was pointed out to me very clearly. I had just had my airplane through one of its yearly inspections called "annuals." We use these inspections as times during which we have regular maintenance completed, as well as taking care of any problems that seem to crop up. I had been told that the brakes needed a minor repair, which I authorized right away. Shortly after the work had been done, and the annual completed, I was on a trip to Houston, Texas to pick up my parents. On the trip home, I landed at El Dorado, Arkansas for fuel. While taxiing out for takeoff, a violent shimmy began, and I nearly lost control of the aircraft before bringing it to a stop. Inspection revealed that the brakes had been repaired improperly. Had the brakes failed at a higher speed, a serious accident could have occurred.

Now consider the owner of the shop who repaired the brakes. He had not participated in the repair. I'm not even sure that he looked at the airplane while it was in his hangar. His employees had done the work, good or bad. But if I had sued, (which I did not do) I would have sued the owner, not the employee! One way to cover this is through different types of insurance, but that can be extremely expensive and can still leave you with serious exposure.

Incorporating using the Sub S type of structure is little better because all corporate income and most of the liability flows down to your IRS Form 1040 at tax time. Additionally, the income is still treated as earned, so again, you have the self-employment tax question with which to deal. A final, though no less important consideration is probate.

I hope I'm not the first to break this news to you, but we are all going to die. When we do, someone will have to deal with the things we leave behind. Some of these things can be dealt with fairly simply. Our more personal possessions—clothes, jewelry, et cetera—simply pass on to others usually through a will or trust. Some items, homes, autos, airplanes, business interests, stock, et cetera, are far more difficult to dispose of and will require the courts to get involved. This is called "going through probate." Think about it this way. If something you leave behind has a title, or deed, or other form of legally defined ownership requiring someone's signature to pass on this ownership, the courts have to get involved because you are no longer around to sign anything! This probate process will require time to complete and fees must be paid to the court and various lawyers for spending this time to handle details that you could have taken care of before you left this life! Additionally, there can be huge federal (and state?) estate taxes, which must be paid.

If most of your estate was non-liquid, that is little cash and lots of hard assets, then your heirs could be required to sell a good portion of what you wanted to leave them just to pay these fees and taxes. Considering the tender feelings and possible emotional attachments your family may have for these items. This situation could be a very real hardship on those that you loved and cared for all of your life.

"C" CORPORATIONS

Most, if not all, of these challenges can be effectively handled through a "C" corporation. This is a system that large companies like Boeing and Chevron employ, and with good reason. We can use the examples set by these companies as patterns for structuring our own businesses, even if we never see ourselves growing to their size and scope. The reason for pursuing this is to enable us to use a corporation to help us gain the same benefits as the large companies do. Think about it. If Sub S corporations or sole proprietorships were the best way to do business, isn't it reasonable to assume that the large companies would be using them? But they don't! They use C corporations, trusts, foundations, and other entities.

From now on, I'll refer to the C corporation simply as a corporation. When you create a corporation, you create an entirely new person or entity, having a life and identity of its own. The federal government recognizes them in that way. They are even required to have their own tax or employer identification numbers. They are eternal. A corporation cannot die unless you kill it! When you create it, you can own all of it, part of it, or none of it. An important point here is that you can control it even if you don't own it!

For some, corporate structuring can be very complex and may require a good team of legal and tax experts to help guide you in setting it up. For most of us, however, it is a simple process to set up two or three entities, which can then be used to legally shelter future income from excessive taxation and liability.

As an air traffic control specialist, my salary was taxed much like yours. All of my income was earned. I paid social security and federal income taxes based upon the $70,000 compensation package I received each year. I had the typical deductions most Americans use, which brought my taxable income down to a point where I was paying about $18,000 per year in taxes. Most of what I spent money on was not tax deductible. That was because I was not involved in a business. I was simply an employee with no business income whatsoever. Consequently, my expenses were, by definition, personal expenses, and therefore not tax deductible.

When I began trading in the stock market, I realized that I was about to start making more money than I had ever imagined. If I personally earned $200,000 in the stock market, that figure would be added to my FAA salary and I would be paying taxes somewhere up in the 39% bracket. That would have amounted to around $80,000 in taxes! I needed some help is determining how to handle this challenge. I decided to attend a class to learn how to use corporations and other entities. Let me show you some of the things I learned, which I now teach.

Because it is a business, a corporation has at least two advantages that an individual does not. First, it has a lower tax rate. On income up to $50,000, corporations will pay 15% in income taxes compared to around 26% for individuals. That is a savings of around $6,000 if you can shift that income from yourself to a corporation. Of course there is a charge for the incorporation process, but it is nowhere near $6,000, and you only pay the setup costs once. You keep the tax savings forever. As your income increases above $50,000, you can shift that extra income to a different corporation to theoretically keep each entities' income below $50,000. If your income continues to rise, a nice problem to have by the way, you can continue to create new entities.

REDEFINE WHAT YOU SPEND

The second advantage of incorporating has to do not with what you earn, but what you spend. As individuals, we have a severely limited number of tax deductions. Corporations do not suffer the same situation, however. They can deduct any and all expenses as long as they are legitimate business expenses. What are legitimate business expenses? Almost whatever you want them to be! It really depends upon intent. Why did the business spend that money? Was it in the line of business? If so, then deduct it. Let's take a quick time out on that one. Don't ever cheat on your taxes!! If you do, you will get caught. And it won't be pleasant. Besides, it is not necessary. There are so many legal ways to save on taxes that it just doesn't make sense to take such chances. Also, you should never go back and try to turn personal expenses into business deductions. Again, it's not worth the risk. I don't want to turn this book into a study of the IRS code, but it may be helpful to look at a few ideas.

Take a look at where you are presently spending your money. A good source of information is your checkbook. Go back over your last two or three check registers and make a list of where your money is going. You will find the typical fixed expenditures such as your house payment or rent, your car payment or other categories depending upon your particular situation. Are you spending for other things like your children's allowance, entertainment, clothing, education, et cetera?

Notice that most of your money is spent on items which are not tax deductible. Why are these expenses not deductible? Because they are personal expenses. Why not turn these into business expenses? Here are a few ideas.

First, start two or three corporations. Let one of these companies be a leasing company. Move most of your hard assets such as cars, boats and real estate into this corporation. You will have to actually re-title these assets into the name of that corporation. You will no longer own them, the corporation will. Now let this corporation lease these things to you or another of your corporations, which will in turn, provide them to you for your use as an employee. The leasing corporation can now begin to depreciate the value of these items to offset the income it receives from the lease payments. The second corporation can write off the amount of the monthly lease as a legitimate business expense. Notice that you are now able to legally deduct the cost of your car or home inside one or more of the corporations. You have created legitimate business-related tax deductions from previously non-deductible personal expenses. Let me give you an example of one of the things I'm doing.

My family and I began a leasing company using the C type corporation structure. This was the second corporation we began. We moved all hard assets, including all cars, the one surviving airplane and the rental house into the corporation. Additionally, the company picked up another piece of real estate. It is a beautiful home in a really prestigious part of the city. It is about 5,000 square feet, three levels, with a split-level deck surrounding a huge swimming pool in a back yard, which is surrounded by an eight-foot privacy fence. Can you guess which house we are living in? That's right. We no longer occupy the small rental house, but have now moved up to the "big house!" However, we are still renters. We rent this house from the leasing company. We actually write them a check each month. That's important—keep everything on a solid business foundation.

We now rent this house from one corporation and sublease office space on the 2nd floor to another corporation.

Now we are subletting office space to another corporation. They actually write us a check every month. At the same time that we are paying rent to one corporation, we are collecting rent from another corporation! Is it possible to rent the home for say, $1,000 per month and sublet the office space for say, $2,000 per month and walk away with a profit? Why do something like this? Here are two reasons:

1. **By renting out office space to a separate corporation, you are avoiding the red flag of in-home office deductions. You are not claiming a deduction, you are claiming additional income!**
2. **By subletting for more than you have to pay for the house, you are creating income for yourself. Most importantly, this additional money is unearned passive rental income. You don't pay FICA on unearned income. Maximize this one!**

If you take these ideas to their ultimate conclusion, you can eventually own nothing and yet control everything. And that is precisely the point. This is so important that I spend a full day of class time talking about just these kinds of ideas.

Here's another idea. Do you presently own any life insurance? Who is typically the owner of such policies? Right, the insured or his or her spouse. Are the premiums deductible? No! This is a personal expense. Why not make a corporation the owner and beneficiary of your policy. The premiums, in most instances, can now be considered a deductible business expense.

For additional ideas, let me suggest a good reference book. Get a copy of *Brilliant Deductions*, by Wade B. Cook. This is a 200 page book packed with methods of turning personal expenses into business deductions.

The bottom line then is to carefully structure your entire life using legal entities. Do nothing in your own name. Own nothing but control everything! Don't trade in a personal account. Rather, open various corporate accounts, at least one for each corporation or entity. The profits from these trades belong to the corporation, which can in turn pay for those things on which you are presently spending money on a personal, non-deductible level.

CHAPTER 5

PUTTING IT ALL TOGETHER

How do you actually put all of this information together and begin running your business on a profitable basis? I want to make an important point here. Do not allow yourself to become overwhelmed by all of this information. We've covered many of the business basics and will shortly describe how each of the strategies can work. All of this new information is going to seem really intimidating at first. Is it really possible to master all of the knowledge necessary to make these strategies work for you within a prudent business plan? It is not only possible, but is easier than you might imagine. While attending my first class on the stock market, I understood very little of what was going on. You may have heard that there are three types of people; those who *make* things happen, those who *watch* things happen, and then the people like me, who wonder *what happened?*

Although my knowledge level was far from what I wanted it to be, I saw the trades that the instructor was making and knew that at least *he* understood what he was doing. Knowing that someone else was making this work for them gave me the motivation I needed to make it work for me as well. As I watched my classmates actually trading and making money, I realized that you don't have to be an expert to make money in the stock market. To be sure, there is work involved in learning the strategies, but once those are mastered through some study and a lot of practice, the barriers to generating cash come crashing down. And more importantly, the barriers stay down. Once you gain the knowledge, it cannot be taken from you!

Think about someone you might know who does really well in the stock market. If no one comes to mind, consider famous investors like Warren Buffett or Peter Lynch. If they were to lose all of their money today, would they remain penniless for the rest of their lives? Or could they build those fortunes again, rather quickly? I maintain that they would be wealthy again in a very short period of time! What then is the one thing they have, which you presently may lack? That's right, knowledge, information and perhaps some experience.

Your business plan should *begin* with acquiring the knowledge, which has enabled so many others before you to succeed. So how do you get the knowledge? How do you get the information? What you do is up to you, but I decided to become a student of the market. I attended every class I could. I read every book I could. The students who come through my classes are amazed at how much of a financial impact just a little knowledge can have. It is not unusual at all to see some of these students earn from several hundred to several thousand dollars right in class. This happens after they have knowledge about how these strategies work. The underlying theory here is that the more information you have, the more money you are likely to make.

Whatever it takes, learn as much as you can as quickly as you can. Once you have the knowledge, trade everyday to turn that knowledge into a mastered skill! If you have very limited funds with which to begin, practice trade until you are making *more* paper money than you are *losing*.

GET ORGANIZED

We each have different demands our lifestyles have placed upon us. Schedules, family or outside obligations and responsibilities and differing ability levels are all conditions that must be evaluated and controlled any time we begin a new activity in earnest. Starting and successfully running this business will require that you be able to devote *regular* amounts of time to it. I don't care how well you understand the strategies, making money in the market demands concentration and attention to the details.

CONTROL YOUR TIME

At the outset, plan to spend at least two to three hours per day at this. Initially most of this time will be spent in reading, listening to, or watching reference material and studying the strategies. Gradually, you will be able to study less and trade more. Look carefully at your present time constraints and plan in advance when you will be able to devote time to your business.

When I first started working in the stock market on a *part-time* basis, the greatest challenge I faced was finding the time to actually make the trades. I worked during most market business hours, and I found it difficult to actually keep up with the market when it was open. To help with this, I changed my hours. I began to work mostly evenings. This enabled me to study strategies and research potential deals for an hour or so after returning home from work. After a good night's rest, I would be up at the market open, ready to trade any deals I found the previous evening. I would watch CNBC and follow the market for the first hour or so after it opened. I used this early part of the trading day to call the broker for anything I may have missed on CNBC and placing my trades for the day. Most of these trades, by the way, were usually placed within the first hour and a half of the market opening.

When I started working in the stock market on a *full-time* basis, the challenges I faced changed in nature. Now I was confronted with developing the self discipline to stay on task when working. This is easy when you have a supervisor watching over your shoulder telling you what to do and when to do it. It becomes a much more difficult proposition when all of a sudden after 30 years *you* are your *own* supervisor! I had to set regular office hours for myself. I would be up at 6 A.M., watching CNBC until the market opened at 8:30 A.M. My trading time was usually between 8:30 A.M. and 10:00 A.M. I would then break until around 2:00 P.M. I would use that last hour of the market day to review my positions, make any closing trades, and generally make a note of how the market had performed that day and what it was likely to do the next. As a result, I was only spending between two and four hours per day "on the job." I had never had so much free time, and had to be careful to make a conscious effort to show up to work every day at the same time.

The point here is a simple one. When you start doing this as a business, be prepared to face some of the same challenges. While you are still working at your present job, you'll have to create the time to stay abreast of what's going on in the market. One way to do this is to use a stock market information pager. These beepers will alert you to developing trading opportunities. You will most likely need a cell phone if you want to take advantage of these opportunities. Be prepared for your employer's possible reluctance to allow you to conduct your business on company time. You may have to devise some rather creative methods of dealing with your particular situation.

OFFICE SPACE

You will need to have an office in your home from which you can conduct business. I would strongly recommend *against* putting that office in a corner of an existing room, which is being used for other things. It is important that no activities other than those directly related to your business take place in your office. This not only helps you to develop the proper mental attitude or mindset while working (or studying), but also really makes it easy to prove your office-related business expenses at tax time. Remember that you are probably going to be renting that office space to your corporation, so keep everything on a solid business footing. You should allow no personal activities within your corporate offices. To help with this challenge, if possible, choose a separate room for your office. A big storage closet works best. After all, what else are you going to be able to do in a big closet? Additionally, such an arrangement can help you get past losing the guestroom or den.

OFFICE EQUIPMENT

Once you have chosen a site for your office, you are going to need to put a few things in it. First, make sure to have it wired for cable television. If you don't already have one, buy a small color television set so you will be able to monitor CNBC while you work. It should be placed out of the way, but where it can be seen from your workspace. I went down to a local home improvement store and purchased a metal swing-away wall mount similar to what you see in some hospitals or motels. It cost around $35 and saved me both space and another piece of furniture on which to set the television. By the way, your cable television bill is now tax deductible!

Next, have a separate telephone line installed. You will not need extra services such as call forwarding. Certainly *do not* have call waiting! This telephone line will be dedicated to your computer modem for updating stock charts and using on-line internet services. Optional but very desirable is a plain paper fax machine. It connects to the phone line between the outlet and the computer. A phone set should also be connected to the correct outlet on the back of your computer. Among other things, this enables your broker to either call you or fax you information on stocks and account positions. I went to the local office store and purchased a used, reconditioned plain paper fax, copier and printer for around $300 and have never regretted it. An extra phone hand set should cost no more than around $20.

Keep your office furnishings as simple as possible. You will need a desk. Avoid the temptation of buying large, expensive units. They look nice, but can eat up a lot of cash. This is workspace. Your desk should be large enough to accommodate your computer, a printer and some in and out baskets, and still leave you with room to work. Some of my students opt for an inexpensive, six or eight-foot-long table with folding legs. I have two of these in my own office. While they may not make fashion decor statements, they are both cost effective and functional.

Some type of office filing system is necessary. I opted for the small, inexpensive, rollaway hanging-file holders. Filing cabinets are probably too bulky and I didn't like the fact that they were stationary. It is really handy to be able to roll the hanging files over to your desk when you need them and roll them out of the way when you finish with them.

REQUIRED READING

One last piece of equipment to put into your office is a bookcase. You will use this to store all of your reference materials when you are not reading them. Let me suggest some authors you might want to collect and read.

Warren Buffet and Peter Lynch have written several good books on the stock market. Wade B. Cook has written a few, which I consider required reading. These include *Wall Street Money Machine*, *Stock Market Miracles* and *Bear Market Baloney*. Of course, you are now reading one of the most important books to help you get started, this one! All of these books are directly related to your trading in the market. There is another area in which you need to prepare and that is your mindset.

Most people don't succeed because along with other reasons, they are not prepared to succeed mentally. Being in business for yourself requires more than just good business skills, it requires the proper mindset. Read *The Strangest Secret,* by Earl Nightingale. From this book you will learn that you *will* become *whatever you think about all day long.* If you want to become a trader, what should you think about all day long? I've already mentioned *Think and Grow Rich,* by Napoleon Hill. Herein are listed 16 learned characteristics of successful people, which you will want to begin to adopt for yourself.

CORPORATE BROKERAGE ACCOUNTS

Early on, you're going to have to begin to pull as much money together as you can. This will be the money with which you will begin trading. Each of us begin at different financial levels. As previously mentioned, I started with $6,000, and quickly searched around to find an additional $50,000. Remember, I really sacrificed to get my money together. You may already have plenty with which to start. However much it is and whatever the source, put this money in a corporate brokerage account. If you don't have one, your broker will gladly help you with this. *Don't trade in your own personal account.* This is a business, so treat it like one! If you put personal funds into a corporate brokerage account, you have just lent money to a corporation. Draw up appropriate loan documents. You might want to consider taking your first year's personal income needs out of the corporation as return of a loan. Doing this might enable you to have $0 personal, taxable income during the first year or so of doing business!

BANK ACCOUNTS

In Chapter 4, I talked about structuring your business with corporations or other entities, and using a good tax and legal team to help you do it correctly. Once you have this done, be sure to open bank accounts for each of those entities. It is important that you pay *all* bills through these accounts. *Do not mix* personal and business funds! This may seem like a daunting task at first, but as you begin to redefine what you are now personally spending as business related, start to pay these bills quickly from one of the business accounts. Stay on track with this, keeping all receipts and maintaining spotless records. Don't be surprised if it takes you a year or so to get used to this!

CREDIT CARDS

It is always a good idea for the business to have its own credit card. The bookkeeping is so much simpler as most corporate card accounts receive expense breakdowns by category. As soon as your company can get approved, get a corporate card from one of the major card companies (I like American Express), and use this as the primary means of paying your bills. Never, never make a personal purchase on a company card! There will be additional charges for the corporate cards, so don't let this surprise you. Charges range from less than $50 to over $100 per year, depending on the company.

IN SUMMARY

Each year, I teach hundreds of students to do what I have been able to do. Whether they attend one of my live two-day workshops, watch my home-study videos, or listen to my audio courses, I'm gratified by the number of students who go on to change their lives forever. I receive letters almost daily from grateful students who have been able to set themselves financially free from the routines which previously held them to standards, and conditions, which were beyond their control. It is my earnest hope that this book will inspire you in some small way to stretch beyond your imagined limits to do something special with your life. If so, then my goal has been attained.

Before moving into the actual market strategies, my final word for you is *never give up!* Keep plugging away at this and don't ever give up. Do not allow negative friends or relatives to talk you out of your dreams, whatever they may be. Do not allow the market to beat you up to the point where you quit. You'll want to often enough, but hang in there! To be totally non-original, "I never said it would be easy, just ... worth it!"

With some of these business basics out of the way, let's now move into the strategies, which I use for *Making A Living In The Stock Market...*

SECTION
II

MARKET
STRATEGIES

CHAPTER 6

BASIC STRATEGIES

$\mathbb{T}$he most basic strategy we'll discuss is buying stock. You should always have a reason for buying stock other than just buying stock. If you are going to make this a business, one key to success is know why you are buying the stock. The prevailing mentality of most brokers is to buy the stock and hold it for long-term growth. As with any other business, everything you do, every trade you make needs to be done for the sole purpose of generating cash. There are a few of rules to keep in mind.

The first rule is to never buy stock if you can't see a quick profit. Look at the chart for Allied Signal (ALD) one the next page. The separation in the price graph shown in September is a stock split. What I want you to pay attention to is what has happened since the split. Notice that in October, the stock price slipped from the low $40s to the mid to high $30s. Pay close attention to what began to happen in early February. The price began a steady rise back to the $40s. The stock was on weakness and has begun to strengthen. A good time to buy the stock would have been in late January as it began its climb. You could have bought the stock for around $38 and sold it two weeks later for around $41, netting a $3 per share profit.

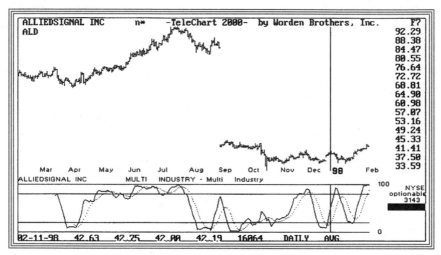

Allied Signal showing a great buying opportunity in late January

The second rule is to buy low and sell high Only buy when the stock price is on a dip! I buy stock only for one of two reasons. One is to resell it quickly at a higher price, generating a spendable profit. The other reason is to use the stock itself as a cash-generating machine through covered calls, which we'll discuss later. My point is simple. If buying stock will not result in a rapid generation of cash, I don't buy it!

CAPITAL GAINS

A profit resulting from the sale of stock (or options) can be considered a capital gain and thus unearned income. This is the kind of income you want to maximize! The major advantage of unearned income is that it is not subject to social security taxes, which can amount to around a 15% loss. An additional source of potential profit from owning stock is income received in the form of dividends. Keep in mind that not all stocks pay a dividend and that these dividends are usually too small to be considered a significant cash generator.

CASH FROM STOCKS GOING NOWHERE - "CHANNELING"

Sometimes stocks move up for a while and then down for a while with such regularity that they appear to "channel" between predictable highs and lows. The stock appears to be going nowhere, but these movements can be extremely profitable if we are astute enough to recognize them. Look at the chart for Wal-Mart on the next page. This picture should give you a graphic idea of what a channeling stock looks like. Notice how often the stock price movement changes direction. These changes give the chart a "sawtooth" appearance.

Look specifically at the last quarter, annotated "OND," of 1993, that is just before the "94." The stock began trading around $24, rose to a high of almost $30, and then fell back to around $24. Note what happened during the first quarter of 1994. This stock price movement was repeated almost to the exact values! This is a great example of a stock channeling between two predictable values, a support of $24 and a resistance of around $29. Had you purchased 1,000 shares at $24 in October of 1993, you could have sold it at around $29 in November and made around $5,000 before commissions. This could have been repeated, almost to the penny, during the next quarter. Had you played both of these, you would have earned around $10,000 in profits during that six-month period of time!

I didn't notice Wal-Mart stock's channeling behavior until the third quarter of 1995. I bought 100 shares around $21 and waited until it moved up to around $24 at which time I sold it. Sensing a potential pattern for profit, the next time it fell to around $21, I bought another 100 shares. My total cost each time was around $2,100 plus commissions. Within a few weeks, the stock was back up to around $24. I sold the stock around $24 1/4 and twice realized a profit of around $300.

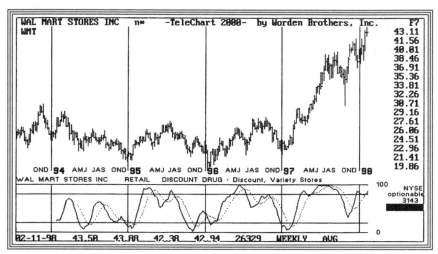

Wal-Mart Stock demonstrated a great channeling opportunity

If you find a stock with this type of predictable behavior, buy it at the lower value. As soon as you are filled, that is as soon as you are notified that you have purchased the stock, place a GTC (Good Til Cancelled) order to sell it at the higher value. If the stock channels with a predictable regularity, you should have a rough idea of when you should be able to sell it and what price you will get for it. Do this as often as the stock repeats this behavior and you have a cash generating money machine!

Let me take another time out to talk about yield. In its most basic form, yield can be quickly and simply calculated by dividing the profit you made on a trade by the original amount you had to invest to do the deal. For example, when I bought Wal-Mart at $21 and then sold it at $24 1/4, I had a profit of $3 1/4 (not counting commissions) on an investment of $21. If you divide $3.25 by $21, you get 15.4%. This represents a phenomenal return for a few weeks!

Looking at yield in this way can lead us to even greater profits through increased leverage. Suppose Wal-Mart stock had been channeling between $5 and $8 1/4. If I had bought it at $5 and sold it at $8 1/4, I would have realized the same $3 1/4 profit, but look at the yield. $3.25 divided by my cost of $5 would be a yield of 65%! The premise here should be obvious. Look for cheaper stocks with this type of movement. Try to restrict yourself to stocks between $3 and $10. This keeps a smaller amount of money tied up and can offer up some remarkable returns.

INCREASED LEVERAGE WITH STOCK OPTIONS

This principle of increased leverage is extremely important and you must understand it thoroughly if you are to maximize your returns in the stock market. When I left the FAA after only two months of trading experience, my only strategy was in writing (selling) covered calls.

Before you can understand how covered calls work, you must have a clear understanding of options and how they offer a marvelous way to increase your leverage on your money! Let's look at some basic features of options. Those of you who are experienced option traders might want to skip to the next chapter.

By way of definition, an option is a right to either buy or sell shares of stock. Options are purchased in the same way stock is purchased, that is through a broker/market maker using the quote system. A "call" is the right to buy stock while a "put" is the right to sell stock. If you own a call you own the right to buy stock. Conversely, if you own a put, you own the right to sell stock, even if you don't presently possess the stock. You can buy and sell options just as you would stock.

Calls and puts have "strike prices," which dictate the price at which the stock may be bought and sold. For example, owning a $45 call on Coca-Cola stock gives you the right to buy that stock at $45. Owning a $35 put on Ford gives you the right to sell Ford stock at $35 per share. Buying and selling stock with options is referred to as "exercising your option."

Not all stocks have options and usually no stocks priced below $5 are "optionable." So strike prices start at $5 and increase in $2.50 increments until reaching $25. Between $25 and $200, strike prices increase in $5 increments. Above $200, strike prices are multiples of $10. For example, assume that General Motors (GM) is priced around $63. We could purchase the right to buy GM stock at $60 by buying a GM $60 call. We could not however, purchase a GM $61 call because between $25 and $200, strike prices are multiples of $5.

All options do something that no stock does. They expire. That is, an option is good for only a limited period of time. The date on which an option expires is determined by its "expiration date," which becomes a part of how we name options. For example, the GM August $60c (note that the word "call" has been replaced with a small "c") will expire in August. All options expire on the 3rd Friday of their expiration month, whatever month that might be. This expiration feature is what makes options so dangerous to trade. If we don't buy enough time, that is if we don't buy options out far enough into the future, the stock might not have enough time to behave as we want it to and our options might expire worthless.

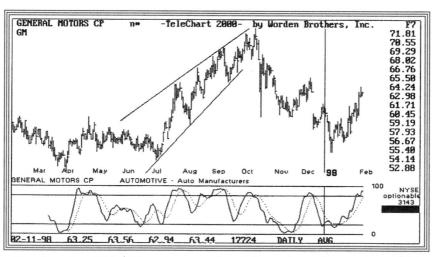

Buying the GM $60c gives us the right to buy the stock at $60

We purchase stock in shares, but we purchase options in "contracts." One contract controls 100 shares of stock. Ten contracts then control 1,000 shares of stock. We can buy as few as one contract or as many as we wish. Prices on these contracts are quoted on a per share basis. Say the quote on the GM August $60c is 3 ½ (bid) x 3 ¾ (ask). If we wanted to buy one contract of this option, we would have to pay $375 plus commissions. That is, 1 contract x 100 shares per contract x $3.75, or $375. Don't forget that we must buy at the "ask" price.

By the same reasoning, ten contracts would cost $3,750. Selling options works much the same way except that we would be selling at the "bid" price of $3.50 per share. So selling one contract would bring in $350 while ten contracts would earn $3,500. The money, which we pay or receive whenever we buy or sell options, is called "premium."

Premium consists of two components, "intrinsic value," and "extrinsic," or more commonly called "time value." The sum of the intrinsic value and the time value will always equal the premium. Intrinsic value is simply the difference between the stock price and the strike price, or zero, if the difference is a negative number. A more simple way to grasp this idea is to pretend that we are going to exercise our option to buy the stock (or to sell if we own a put). Using our GM example from above, note that the stock is presently selling for $63. The August $60c gives us the right to buy the stock for $60.

Let's say we exercise this call and we now own the stock. How much did it cost us? That's right, $60, because that is what the strike price guaranteed us, the right to purchase the stock for $60. Now that we own the stock at $60, we could sell the stock in the open market for $63, thereby netting a profit of $3 per share, not counting commissions and the cost of the option. This $3 profit is intrinsic value. Because there is intrinsic value, the August $60c is said to be "in the money." Note that the premium for the August $60c was $3.75. If the intrinsic value is $3, then by definition, the time value must be 75¢ ($3 intrinsic + 75¢ time value = $3.75 premium). This relationship will become important when we begin to study various strategies.

Consider another call on the same stock. Let's say the GM August $65c was quoted at 1 ¼ x 1 ½. What is the intrinsic value of this call? If the stock were selling at $63, the difference between the $63 stock price and the $65 strike price is -$2, giving zero intrinsic value since it is a negative number. If the intrinsic value is zero, then the time value must be equal to the entire premium of $1.50. Remember that the sum of the intrinsic and time values equals the premium! That is, 0 + $1.50 = $1.50. This is an "out-of-the-money call." An easier way to remember this is that any time the call's strike price is greater than the stock price, the call is said to be out of the money. Conversely, if the strike price is less than the stock price, the call is in the money. These relationships are reversed when considering puts. Finally, "at-the-money" options (calls and puts) have strike prices equal to the stock price.

It is important to understand how option premiums change. Let's stay with our GM example above. If GM stock remains at $63 per share, the intrinsic value, $3, of the August $60c (or any other in-the-money strike price) will not change. The time value, however, decays constantly. In my classes, I like to use the example of an ice cube. It begins to melt away as soon as you remove it from the freezer and will continue to melt more and more rapidly until it finally disappears! Time value does exactly the same thing. It begins to erode as soon as the option is written, and this erosion accelerates, particularly during the last two weeks before its expiration date. In trading options, try to avoid holding an option much beyond the last two weeks prior to that third Friday. In our example, the August $60c had an intrinsic value of $3 and a time value of 75¢. This 75¢ will decay away to zero by the third Friday, so the premium at that time will be whatever the intrinsic value is, at least until the market closes. After the close, the option is said to have expired and will be worthless! Think about how much more rapid premium decay could be in an out-of-the-money call since it has no intrinsic value! On that third Friday, the premium could be very close to zero even before the close of the market.

GET GOOD AT THE BASIC STRATEGIES

In order to fully appreciate how powerful some of the more advanced strategies can be, you need to become completely familiar with how to use these basic plays. When buying stock, only buy when the stock price is in a pull back. Look for and be sensitive to those stocks whose charts suggest a channeling pattern. When you become proficient at buying stock on weakness and selling it on strength, move over to the more highly leveraged technique of trading options, puts and calls, on these very same situations. That is, when a stock price is low and moving up, buy a call. When a stock price is high and moving down, buy a put. This sounds simple and it really is, but there is no substitute for practice, so let me introduce you to a method of trading, which is as close to being risk free as you can come.

PAPER TRADING

I am going to assume that in the beginning we all start with a finite amount of cash with which to trade. If you have an unlimited supply of cash, then good for you. However, the rest of us will probably be working with amounts which will limit the number of trades we are able to do. In short then, most of us will run out of money before we run out of deals. That is, at some point in time, we will have all of our assets tied up in one or more of several trades. At that point, we will be waiting until some of our cash is freed up by our being able to close out one or more of our positions. Now, how does having all of our money obligated affect our trading?

In my classes, I teach that there are three principles, which are keys to success in the stock market: knowledge, practice and repetition. When we run out of money, does that affect our knowledge? Of course not. That's why most of us are willing to pay a tuition to attend class. Once you gain the knowledge you will have it forever! But consider the second key, practice. If we run out of money, our practice must stop. And how does that affect the third key, repetition? Likewise, it stops until we once again have more cash with which to trade. In other words, when you run out of money and must stop trading, you lose two of the three keys to becoming a successful trader!

To avoid this, I encourage my students to "paper trade." That is, to research and track a trade just as if you actually put money into the deal. Paper trading is perhaps the single best way to gain the practice, repetition, and experience necessary to become proficient at these trades without being devastated by the mistakes, which will inevitably occur.

I feel so strongly about this that I have developed paper trading exercise sheets and included them in Appendix 1 of this book. As we go through each strategy, before putting any money into the market, paper trade each strategy over and over again.

If paper trading is to be a benefit to you, it is vital that each trade you do, each position you open, be followed until you can close it out. This may mean that you have to call your broker several times each day. Whatever you have to do, follow the play until it is over. At that time, complete the bottom of the trade sheet wherein you calculate your profit or your loss. Once you are making more money than you are losing, then you are ready to start trading real money.

CHAPTER

OPTION PRINCIPLES

$\mathbb{H}$ow do you make money on options? The answer is elegantly simple, buy low and sell high! I'm not trying to be cute here. That is exactly what I do, buy low and sell high. (And not always in that order.) Understand this, I, like most other option traders, buy options to sell them at a profit. I never buy a call to buy the stock. I never exercise my options. It is much more effective to consider them inventory and sell them profitably whenever I can! Let's use a trade I made some time ago as an example. Monsanto (MTC) announced a five-for-one stock split. The stock was trading around $132 at the time of the announcement in March of 1996. I purchased 10 of the June $150c at $6. Do you remember how to compute how much money I spent? Ten contracts x 100 shares per contract x $6 per share = $6,000.

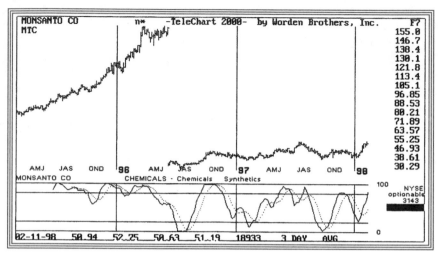

When Monsanto announced a 5:1 stock split it soared to $155

As is common with most stock split announcements, MTC stock began to go up. It moved from $132 to around $138, or about a 5% increase. At the same time, the premium on my June $150c moved from $6 to around $10, or about a 66% increase! MTC stock continued to rise to around $150, an 8% rise, and the premium on the June $150c moved up to $16, or another 60% increase. I hope you noticed what happened here. A 5% rise in the stock generated better than a 60% rise in the option's premium. Then another 8% rise in the stock produced an additional 60% rise in the premium.

All of this occurred in less than two hours, and I sold my June $150c with a $10 per share profit. On 10 contracts, that's a $10,000 profit! Did you notice how a relatively small increase in the price of the stock produced a huge increase in the value of the premium? It is this relationship between stock price movement and option premium movement, which allows you to generate huge profits when dealing with options. I played the options, but they are risky. Should I have played the stock?

To purchase 1,000 shares of MTC, I would have spent around $132,000, a tidy sum! I could have sold the stock later that day for $150,000 and netted $18,000. Rather than tying up such a large sum of money, I decided to buy the June $150c for $6 per share (which is

$6,000 for 10 contracts). Two hours later, I sold the June $150c and walked away with a $10 per share profit, which amounts to $10,000 profit on 10 contracts. Yes, I would have made an additional $8,000 on the stock play, but I more than doubled my money on the option. The difference is leverage. Instead of trading stock at $132 per share, trade the option at $6 per share.

As different stocks move up, options on these stocks will move up at different rates. But there is always one constant upon which you can rely. On a percentage basis, if the stock moves up a little, the option will move up a lot.

NEWS MOVES

Most of my trades are made because some type of news has been released, which could make the stock move one direction or another. Having access to this news is an absolute necessity. There are many different news sources, which are available, and I use as many as I can. An obvious source is your full-service broker. But you have to let your broker know what you are looking for and then they must agree to call you quickly when news breaks. My brokers have been taught what I am looking for and know immediately what type of deal I'm going to play. I even let some of them make the play for me without getting my permission first. This is called discretion. If your broker is good, don't be afraid to give him some freedom to trade in your account.

Another news source I depend heavily upon is a pager. When news breaks, I get a page, which tells me what the news is. If it is something I want to play, I immediately call my broker to place the trade. There are many on the market today from which to choose. I would recommend avoiding those that report only one type of news such as stock splits. You are going to be trading more than just stock splits, so have a pager that reports all types of news: mergers, acquisitions, upgrades, downgrades, and earnings, to name but a few examples.

The principle, which made my Monsanto play work, is that I bought calls on a stock that was going up in value. I knew in advance that the stock was going to go up, so I bought the call and later sold it for a profit after it had gone up with the stock. The key is to recognize what factors will make the price of a stock move up, and then buy the appropriate option.

So how can you learn what situations make stock prices move? Well, you've taken the first step by reading this book. I will outline a few things to look for and suggest some specific plays to make. But please don't stop here. If you are serious about making your living doing this, treat it professionally. Continue to read on the subject. Attend every class you can. You will get out of this business only what you put into it! Now let's look at some potentially profitable option situations.

EARNINGS

Businesses are started in order to earn money. Those businesses, which are very profitable, will grow and expand and possibly become publicly traded. When that happens, they are required to report their earning to the stockholders. While usually reported in the form of a quarterly report, earnings are often released to various news media for public dissemination. Market analysts follow many of the larger, or more popular companies. These individuals track closely the financial progress and overall fiscal health of the company and many make rec-ommendations about such things as where the stock should be priced and what earnings might be anticipated for the current quarter. In that manner, earnings expectations become a matter of public record. If a company earns more than the expectations, the stock is likely to go up. If it earns less, it is more likely to go down. People who follow the stock closely will sometimes make their own predictions about what the earn-ings report will be. Sometime referred to as "whispers," these rumors can be good indicators of stock price behavior.

When a company reports good earnings, you can reasonably expect the stock to rise in value. If you act quickly enough on the news, you can often make money on the options, more specifically buying calls. Let's take a quick time out here and define two different option strategies, long-term and short-term.

A long-term play involves buying options having expiration dates at least four full months or more in the future. A short-term play is to buy options having expiration dates from one to three full months out. For example, if the current month is October, a short-term option could be November, December, and January, if there is a full month left on the November options. Otherwise, the short-term expirations would be December, January, and February. Long-term expirations could be either February and beyond or March and beyond, depending upon whether we can count November as a full month. Strike prices come into play here also. On short-term options, buy strike prices that are just in the money, that is buy the first strike price in the money. On long-term options, buy strike prices that are just out-of-the-money, or buy the first strike price out of the money. For any movement in the stock price, in-the-money options will move faster than out-of-the-money options. On short-term plays, you don't have much time for the option premium to move up, so you buy in the money because they go up more quickly!

Long-term option plays have more time to allow the stock to do what you want it to do, so we can afford to buy the less expensive out-of-the-money options, thus improving the leverage of options even more. When dealing with options, time can either be your best friend or your worst enemy. One key to making money in options is to be exposed to risk for the shortest time possible. When you buy an option, either long or short-term, be prepared to sell it as soon as you can do so profitably. So why should we even consider a long-term option play? It is called safety. Sometimes the stock will not behave the way you expect it to. In these situations, buying enough time to allow the stock to move could prove to be very inexpensive insurance!

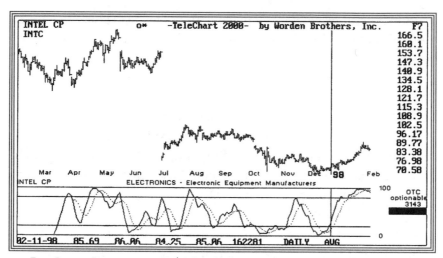

Intel, trading around $85.06 just announced good earnings

When you receive the news that a company has reported better-than-expected earnings, the play is to buy a long-term call on the stock. For example, let's say that Intel, Inc. (INTC) is trading at $85.06 per share and has just reported earnings of $1.25 per share versus expectations of $1.01 per share.

That is really great news. If you can get in before the stock goes up, a play here would be to buy a long-term $90 call. If the current month is October with only two weeks to go in the October expiration month, we would skip October and count out four months to buy the Feb $90c. Suppose you had to pay as much as $5 per share. On 10 contracts, you have just spent $5,000. Now when the stock moves up, the premium on your Feb $90c will go up also. As soon as they are profitable, sell them. Don't hang around waiting for huge profits! Remember, I would much rather make a $1 profit on six deals than to make a $6 (or more) profit from only one deal! In this case, if you can sell your INTC Feb $90c for $6.25 per share, you've just netted a $1.25 per share profit on 1,000 shares (10 contracts). That's a profit of $1,250, or around 22%. Not bad if you can do that in an hour... or a day... or a week... or even a month. But what if the move is a little slow in developing and you have to wait the entire four months to make your profit. Isn't that still a good return?

No! It's a phenomenal return! A return of 22% for a four-month period is equivalent to a 66% annual return, which is unheard of even with the more potent mutual funds.

UPGRADES

When an analyst or brokerage firm follows a stock closely, they will from time to time come out with a rating on the company, or more accurately on the company's stock. In ascending order the most common ratings include: sell, neutral, hold, market perform, market outperform, accumulate, buy, and strong buy. Let's look at what to do with the news when a firm upgrades a stock.

Obviously, the stronger the upgrade, the more the stock is likely to go up. So a change from a hold to a strong buy would really light the stock's fuse. A more likely scenario to trade would be an upgrade from a buy to a strong buy or a market perform to a market outperform. As always, act upon the news as quickly as you can. Before placing the trade, make sure that the stock hasn't already run up. Remember that you don't want to be buying into the tops of these deals. Now, look at this example.

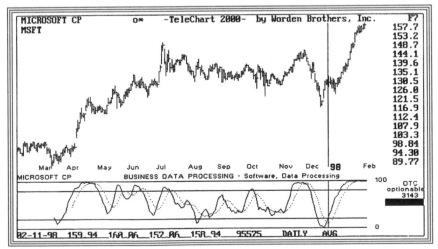

Microsoft (MSFT) trading around $126 upgraded to strong buy

Let's say that Microsoft is currently trading at $126 per share. All of a sudden, Morgan Stanley, a large brokerage firm, raises Microsoft from a buy to a strong buy. If you are able to get in quickly, before the stock runs up, buy a long-term call.

If the upgrade was announced in the month of January, we might go out to May and buy the $130 calls for say, $7 per share. Determine how much profit you want (don't be piggish here) and be prepared to sell these calls as soon as you are profitable. Say you want to make $1 per share profit. When the stock goes up, the premium on your call will go up. When it hits your exit point of $8, sell immediately. The chart shows that this would have happened very quickly.

NEW PRODUCTS

Whenever a company develops a new product, the stock in that company can rise dramatically. This is particularly true if the company is well known and already has a market niche. Iomega (IOM) is a well-known company, which manufactures computer hardware products such as disk drives. Some time ago, they announced the development of a new product called a ZIP Drive. On the next page, look at the actual chart of what happened to Iomega when the announcement of the new disk drive product was announced.

This product had the potential to redefine where and how information was stored on personal computers. Immediately after the announcement, the price of the stock jumped significantly. In April of 1996, you could have purchased the stock for around $17.50 per share. Within a few days, the stock was trading around $53!

This is another long-term play. In April, when the announcement was made, you could have purchased the August $20c for around $5 per share. A few days later, you could have sold those calls for around $13. Keep in mind that even though you bought calls out into August, you don't have to hold them that long. Sell them for an acceptable profit as soon as you can.

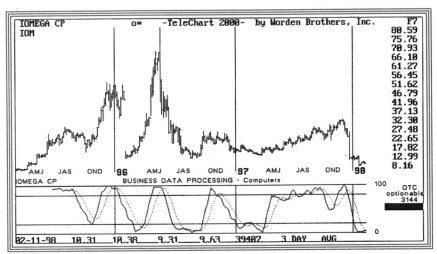

When the zip drive was announced, Iomega (IOM) shot up

ACQUISITIONS

Whenever one company buys another, there is usually a predictable stock movement for each company. The stock of the company being acquired will usually go up while the other will experience a temporary decline. These moves can be very rapid, particularly if the deal involves a cash price at which the new company would be purchased. This is sometimes referred to as a cash "tender offer." In most cases, the play here is to buy a long-term call on the company being acquired.

Be very careful on these deals. Avoid buying in if the stock has already risen sharply. Otherwise, you could find yourself buying in at a premium only to see your investment waste away as the prices naturally settle.

STOCK SPLITS

Whenever a company splits its stock, it usually goes up. In fact, such companies are over 250% more likely to rise than companies who do not split. We can play a stock split company in several different ways, but the important thing to know for now is that a stock split represents a wonderful opportunity to make money because of the intense upward pressure on the price of the stock. This is such an important strategy; I will devote an entire chapter to it later on in the book.

BUYING PUTS ON STOCKS GOING DOWN

When stocks go up, call premiums go up. The reverse is also true, when stocks go down, call premiums go down. However, it is possible to profit when stock prices fall by buying puts. When stock prices go down, put premiums go up. To understand this, you must keep in mind that owning a put gives you the right to force someone to buy stock from you at a predetermined strike price. Let's say that Chrysler (C) stock is trading around $38 per share.

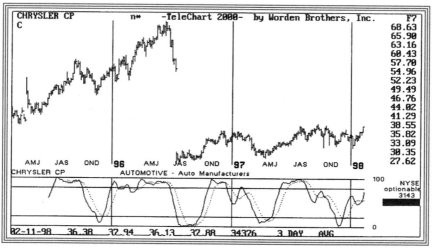

Chrysler (C) is trading around $38 when it loses a lawsuit

Suppose a lawsuit is filed against the auto manufacturer and Chrysler loses. This is really bad news. Which way is the stock most likely to be going? That's right, down! If you get the news quickly enough before the stock has fallen very far, you can buy a long-term put. If this is February, you might want to go out to May and buy the May $35p. Say you have to pay $3 per share. Note here that we have remained within the definition of a long-term option play. We bought a strike price, which was just out-of-the-money. That's right, if the stock is at $38, then the first out of the money put is the $35 strike price. It works just the opposite of calls, doesn't it? Admittedly, this can be confusing. Pretend for a moment that you own a $35 put on a stock selling for $38 per share. The put gives you the right to force someone to buy this $38 stock for $35 (the strike price). There's not much value in owning that put, is there? This is an out of the money put. So the premium is going to be pretty cheap.

Now, let the stock fall to say, $30. Keep in mind what you own if you have the $35 puts. You still have the right to force someone to buy the stock from you at the strike price of $35, don't you? But since the stock has fallen to $30, you can now make a $5 per share profit by buying the stock on the open market for $30 and forcing someone to buy it from you at $35. The put has now become in the money. Is there any value in owning such a put? Of course there is! Now the premium is going to be fairly expensive. Notice that this is the same put that we said earlier was out of the money, of little value and therefore relatively cheap to buy. Now we're saying that it would be pretty expensive to purchase. The strike prices are the same. What is the only thing that has changed? That's right, the stock went down! Any time the price of the stock drops, the put premium will go up. If you had purchased the Chrysler May $35p at $3 per share and the stock falls to $30, you will probably be able to sell that put for around $8, netting a profit of around $5 per share.

What we have covered in this chapter are some of the basic principles of dealing with options. We have defined the two basic options with which we will be working, puts and calls. We have discussed some important considerations of options, concepts such as in-the-money, out-of-the-money, and intrinsic value.

We have defined two basic plays, long-term and short-term, and looked at where they might be valid strategies. While many of the terms and concepts may be new to you, patient study, and practice will make them seem like old friends. A word of caution is in order. Options are extremely risky to trade. Learn to trade them profitably by paper trading until you are thoroughly familiar with their behavior.

CHAPTER 8

CASH GENERATION STRATEGIES

When I first began trading in the market, the first strategy I used was channeling, as I have already described. After attending my first class on stock market strategies, I moved beyond this and began writing covered calls. My returns began to go up to a point where within two months of taking the class, I was making enough money to actually earn a living in the stock market.

The concept of moving beyond your present knowledge or experience level is very important to understand if you are to progress. In any activity in which we are engaged, sports, academic, or financial, you will reach a point where you must move ahead if you are to continue to get better at what you are doing. In college, we take progressively harder and harder courses in order to complete our education. In business, we might expand to more and more locations until we are where we want to be financially. I learned to channel stock by going out and doing it. For me to be able to make more money, I had to attend a class to learn other strategies. I had to move on beyond my present position. Most of the students who attend my classes are there for one reason, to learn additional strategies so they can earn more money. In his book, *Think and Grow Rich*, Napoleon Hill found that the successful people he studied had committed to continue to learn about their chosen endeavor. For most, this was not an inherent characteristic, it was a learned trait! I encourage each of my students to read Mr. Hill's book so they will understand the importance of moving beyond their present position.

WHY DON'T MORE PEOPLE SUCCEED?

All of this may sound rather obvious, but amazingly, most people will not do it. Why is that? Why will most people not apply this simple concept so they can move to the next level? In an interview several years ago, Mr. H.L. Hunt was asked what a person must do to achieve success.

His response was basically fourfold. Paraphrasing, he said, first decide what you want. Then he said decide what you're willing to give up to get it. Third, set your priorities. And finally, he said, "Be about it!" Right here is where the vast majority of people doom themselves. They are not willing to sacrifice anything to achieve something better. Neither are most of them willing to commit to that first step. Let me give you a specific example of how this principle worked for me.

When I attended my first class on stock market strategies, I learned about the power of covered calls. My challenge was that I only had around $6,000 to trade, not nearly enough to generate a cash flow sufficient to live on. I determined that I would need at least $50,000 to trade in order to support my family. So my family and I set out to put that money together. We lived in a really nice, large house with some equity, so we sold it and moved into a much smaller, less expensive house. In fact, we went from around 3,500 square feet down to around 1,300 square feet. We were living on top of each other!! I sold some personal possessions, one of them an airplane, which I had built, to raise more money. My family and I made some serious sacrifices in order to raise enough money to begin trading at a higher level. I went into debt to take additional classes to move beyond my present knowledge and skill level. In all, we raised around $50,000 and began our stock market career in earnest. Were the sacrifices worth it? My first month writing covered calls, I earned around $24,000. Within three months, I had earned back everything it had cost me to move my trading to a higher level. Yes, my sacrifice was worth it! Mr. Hunt was exactly right, decide what you want, decide what you're willing to give up to achieve it and then be about it!

WHY COVERED CALLS?

I was attracted to covered calls for two reasons. First, they are easy to understand, and even easier to implement. You have to buy stock (if you don't already own it) and then you have to sell someone the right to buy it away from you at a profit. Second, writing (selling) covered calls is so safe that you can even do them in a self-directed IRA! The strategy is even safer than simply buying stock because while you are spending money to purchase the stock, you receive real, spendable money when you sell the call against your stock. Let me give you an example.

HOW COVERED CALLS WORK

My first covered call was on a company called Copytele, Inc., a company that develops business software applications. In October of 1995, I bought 1,000 shares of the stock which was trading around $11.50 per share. I purchased the stock on margin, which means I only had to come up with 50% of the purchase price, or $5,750. The broker supplied the other $5,750. For that, I had to pay margin interest of about .75% per month.

Once I owned the stock, I sold 10 contracts of the November $12.50c and received a premium of $1.50 per share or $1,500, not deducting commissions. Considering that I had earned $1,500 on a $5,750 investment, I had just realized a 26% return on my money! It is important to note which call I sold on my stock. I bought the stock in October for $11.50 per share and sold the November $12.50c. Notice that I sold the calls for the next month out at the next higher strike price over the cost of the stock.

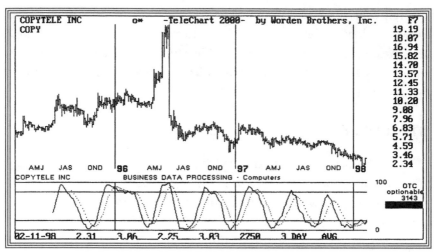

My first covered call was on Copytele (COPY)

When you sell calls against stock you own, you are obligated to hold that stock until the calls expire or until you get called out, or assigned. But that's okay, because your stock is now generating cash you can use for other things like investing or paying bills. When the calls expire, if you are not called out, you are free to write calls again for the next month. If you are called out, you will be paid $12.50 per share (or whatever the strike price is) and you will receive a nice additional profit from the sale of the stock. This, of course, will put you back to a cash position, and you are now free to go out and find another deal.

DETERMINING YOUR RATE OF RETURN

You should be looking for returns of around 10 to 20% per month. These should be relatively easy to find close to the beginning of the call expiration month. As you get deeper into the month, you will find that the premiums will diminish because the time value portion of the premium has started to decay. However, that fact should not affect your overall return. For example, if you were looking for 10% for an entire month, then 5% for only two weeks remaining would be an equivalent return.

To determine what return you will receive on a covered call, simply divide the premium by the stock price. For example, if you pay $9.50 per share for the stock and you can sell the $10 calls for the next month for 75¢ per share, your return is .75/9.50 or 7.8% for the month, not a bad return. Notice that if you are called out, you will make an additional 50¢ per share profit from the sale of the stock. That moves your return up to .75 + .50/9.50, or around 13%. Now do this on margin and your return will double to around 26% because you will not have to spend the entire $9.50 per share, but only $4.75 per share!

To make it easy to remember how to determine your rate of return, you can use the following formula:

$$R = P/S;$$

Where R is your rate of return, P is the call premium you receive, and S is the stock price. If you are called out of your stock, the formula becomes:

$$R = (P+Pr)/S;$$

Where the additional variable "Pr" is the profit (if any) that you receive from the sale of your stock.

SELECTING COVERED CALL CANDIDATES

This all sounds great, but how do you select stocks against which you can write covered calls? Do all stocks qualify? Are there specific characteristics you should look for in the stock? These are all-important questions, so let's look at what makes a stock a good covered call candidate.

There are only two types of stock you ever want to use as covered call candidates: stocks you don't mind owning, and stocks you don't mind selling. Keep in mind that you might have to own them for a while, and you might have to sell them right away.

The first thing to understand is that the stocks have to be optionable. Obviously, you can't sell calls on your stock if the calls don't exist. Next, if you want to double your returns, the stock should be marginable. All of this means that the stocks are probably going to have to be priced at least at $5 per share. Try to keep the price less than around $18 to $20. Buying more expensive stocks can really eat up your supply of cash quickly.

Another way to look at this should illustrate what I'm talking about. You can sell a $100 call on a $100 stock and receive around $1, a 1% return. You can sell a $10 call on a $10 stock and receive around $1, a 10% return. If you were going to earn $1, would you rather tie up $100 or $10? That is, would you rather have a 1% return or a 10% return? You increase your leverage dramatically by writing covered calls on the less expensive stocks.

Regardless of the price, the stock should show signs of going up in value. Remember that you will be selling calls having the next higher strike price than what the stock cost you. If the stock goes up above the strike price, then you will receive profit from the sale of the stock when you get called out.

GENERATING CASH WITH COVERED CALLS

If you choose to begin writing covered calls, how much cash can you reasonably expect to generate? Assuming that you can generate returns of around 10%, beginning with as much as $25,000 will produce $2,500 per month. My experience has shown that by using margin, I can usually average around 20% per month. On $25,000 worth of stock, then, you could earn as much as around $5,000 per month, if you have the same results I have had.

In setting up your trading business, you need to have some idea of how much cash you need to generate each month. That figure will be about 10 to 15% of the total amount of money with which you need to begin. For example, if you need $5,000 each month, you will have between $33,000 and $50,000 with which to start.

GOING NAKED

Covered calls are covered because you own the underlying stock. That is, you own the stock and are prepared to deliver it in the event you are called out. Anyone can be approved to write covered calls because of their relative safety. You can also sell calls against stock that you don't own. This is referred to as going "naked." Notice that this term applies only if you have sold an option. If you were to do so, you would be obligating yourself for considerable risk. For example, suppose you sell $20 calls against stock you don't own. That is, you go naked on a $20 call. Now suppose the stock goes up to $50. You are certain to be called out, but you don't own the stock, so you have to go out into the market and buy the stock at $50 and deliver it at $20. To take on such risk, your broker is going to require you to have more experience trading options. Additionally, he may require you to have more money in your account.

As risky as naked options can be, they can be extremely profitable. Consider what you have to spend to make a trade in naked puts and calls. Nothing! If you are right in the direction you think the stock is moving, your cash outlay in making the trade is absolutely nothing. This means that your rate of return is infinite. If you get good at recognizing stock movement, you can generate unbelievable amounts of cash each month.

NAKED CALLS

Whenever a stock indicates an impending decline, consider selling a short-term naked call. If the stock price does go down below the strike price, you will not be called out, and you will have generated a handsome profit without having purchased anything. Let me show you an example.

Recently Texas Instruments, Inc. (TXN) announced a two for one stock split. The stock was trading around $104 and on the announcement ran up to around $115.

Texas Instruments (TXN) recently ran up on news of a 2:1 split

Experience told me that the stock would probably drop as traders took profits from the recent runup. I sold 10 contracts of a short-term $115 call for around $5. Sure enough, within the next day or so, the stock dropped to around $108. As the stock went down, the premium on the call also went down to around $1.25. Now I had a decision to make. I could wait until the call expired worthless in about 2 ½ weeks and keep the entire $5 for which I had originally sold it, or I could buy it back at $1.25 and net the $3.75 profit immediately. I bought it back and netted $3,750. I made this decision for two reasons.

First, as explained earlier, selling naked options is extremely risky. If the stock had turned and gone back up, a likely possibility for a stock split company, I was likely to have to buy the stock at a higher price and allow myself to get called out at $115. By buying the naked call back, I closed the position, thereby taking my money out of harm's way.

Second, by buying the call back, I freed up a huge amount of money. Let me explain. Whenever you sell a naked option you are exposing yourself to risk. Your stockbroker is going to require that you have enough money in your account to fulfill your obligation to buy the stock in the event it goes up and you are called out. This money is called margin requirement and can be as much as 30 to 50% of your obligated risk.

With a $115 naked call, your broker may require you to put away as much as $60 per share. On 1,000 shares, (10 contracts), your margin requirement could be around $60,000. This money remains in your account, but it is obligated and you cannot use it to trade into other deals until you have closed out that naked position. When I bought the $115 call back, I freed up my margin cash requirement and was able to move quickly on to other trades. Before trading naked options, be sure to check with your broker to see what his margin requirement will be. Also keep in mind that in addition to a lot of cash, your broker will also require that you have a lot of experience in trading options before he will allow you to sell naked options. This is for your protection. You need to understand the risk in any trade and be able to manage that risk.

NAKED PUTS

A less dangerous way to sell naked options is to sell puts. Sell someone the right to sell you stock that you wouldn't mind owning. If you are exercised upon, you will have already taken in the premium from the sale of the put, so you are buying the stock at a discount! Perhaps you could then sell covered calls on your stock. If you are not exercised upon, then you pocketed the premium as profit without having to buy anything. It can be a win-win deal no matter what happens. Let's look at some of the details.

Which stocks qualify for naked put candidates? Any stock that is going up in value. The idea here is to sell an out of the money put. For example, say you find a stock priced around $19 per share. For whatever reason, you believe the stock price is moving up. Sell the $17.50 put for the next month out. Now consider your situation. Someone has just paid you for the right to sell you this stock for $17.50, but the stock is at $19. As long as the stock price remains above $17.50, are they likely to put it to you for $17.50? Of course not. If the stock price remains above the strike price, you are safe and profitable. That's why it is important to do this only on stocks, which are moving up in value. If the stock price stays up until the expiration date, the put will expire worthless and you are ready to move on to another deal.

What is the risk on naked puts? Your financial risk can be an amount equal to the strike price. In the above example, if the stock price fell to zero, you would be put the stock at $17.50. This would result in a loss of $17.50, an amount equal to the strike price of the put you sold!

Obviously, this is an extreme example and I use it only to demonstrate the worst-case scenario. Fortunately, this rarely happens. In any event, your potential risk is the difference between the strike price and whatever the stock falls to. If the stock were to drop to $15, you would have to buy the stock at $17.50. You would therefore be down $2.50 per share ($17.50 - $15 = $2.50). In such a case, you could immediately sell a covered call on the stock to further lower your cost basis in the stock. If the stock were on what you considered a temporary dip, you might want to wait to sell the call until the stock recovered. Waiting until the stock goes back up would result in a higher premium for the call, which translates to higher profits.

Consider your rate of return for a moment. Remember that when you sell naked calls, you don't have to buy anything. The same is true of naked puts. Find a stock that is going up and sell an out-of-the-money put. You take in cash from the sale of the put, and you don't have to spend anything. This means your cost in the deal is zero, giving you an infinite rate of return. That sounds great, but you still have to deal with the margin (cash, in other words), which your broker will require you to keep in your account as long as you are naked.

This margin requirement varies from broker to broker, but 20% is a common amount. That is, your broker will require you to have 20% of the strike price in your account, set aside in the event you were to be put the stock. Additionally, your broker will temporarily set aside the premium you received from selling the put. So you cannot spend the premium until you have closed out your naked position.

If you sell a $17.50 put for say, $1.50, you will tie up 20% of $17.50 or $3.50 per share. For argument's sake, let's agree that our profit is the $1.50 from the put, and our cost is $3.50, our margin requirement. That means our return is $1.50/$3.50 or 42%! This sounds like a phenomenal return, but it's probably lower than what you will actually find in real life. Let me demonstrate.

I'm looking at a copy of the *Wall Street Journal* (see next page). I have turned to the Money and Investing section and found the Listed Options Quotations section. This section lists some of the more active option contracts and their closing prices from yesterday. As I look down the page, I am looking for some lower priced stocks. I find Infrmx, (about one-fifth of the way down the second column—look for the arrows), an abbreviation for Informix (IFMX), which closed at $8.125.

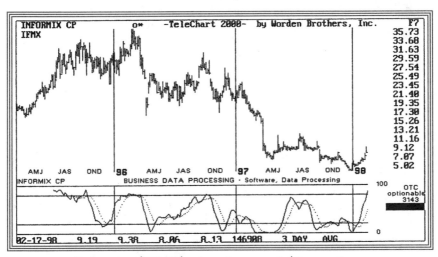

Informix (IFMX) closed around $8 per share

Looking across the column to the right, I see that the March (next month out) $10 puts closed yesterday at $2. If I thought the stock was going to rise to above $10, I could sell the March $10 puts and be relatively safe. Let's suppose I sold 10 contracts. Look at the cash I've generated; 10 contracts at $2 per share will bring in around $2,000 before commissions. How much cash would I have to tie up to do this deal? My margin requirement is 20% of the strike price, so that is .20 x $10, or $2 per share. On 10 contracts, then, I would have a potential profit of $2,000 with a cost of $2,000. This means a return of $2,000/$2,000, or 100%! Of course this only works if I'm right and the stock rises to close above $10 on the third Friday in March, so be sure to do this only on

Option/Strike		Exp.	Call Vol.	Call Last	Put Vol.	Put Last
65 1/4	50	Mar	315	15 1/4	...	...
65 1/4	55	Mar	1260	11 1/2	10	3/4
65 1/4	65	Mar	423	4 1/4	115	3 5/8
DellCptr	10	Feb	2261	3 3/4	1451	2 3/8
111 5/16	10	May	309	12 1/2	77	10
111 5/16	80	Mar	...	...	200	5/16
111 5/16	85	Feb	52	26 1/2	922	1/16
111 5/16	95	Feb	233	16 1/4	1387	5/16
111 5/16	100	Feb	3040	11 7/8	778	7/16
111 5/16	105	Feb	991	7 1/2	1845	1 1/8
111 5/16	105	Mar	296	10 1/2	249	3 7/8
111 5/16	110	Mar	3926	8	238	6 1/2
111 5/16	115	Feb	3627	1 5/8	221	5 1/4
111 5/16	115	Mar	1477	5 5/8	1032	9 3/4
111 5/16	115	May	487	10	...	...
111 5/16	120	Mar	1302	3 3/4	78	[illegible]
111 5/16	120	May	1183	8 1/8	3	[illegible]
DeltaP o	18 3/4	Feb	240	13 3/8	...	...
DeltaAr	115	Feb	206	6 1/2	73	[illegible]
121 1/4	120	Mar	234	6 1/4	30	[illegible]
Dentsp	30	Feb	433	1 5/16	...	...
31 3/16	32 1/2	May	387	11/16	...	...
DiaOff	45	Mar	378	1 13/16	515	[illegible]
Dig Eq	60	Feb	1260	1 3/8	5	[illegible]
60 11/16	60	Mar	1251	2 1/2	...	...
60 11/16	60	Apr	1500	3 3/8	1500	2
60 11/16	65	Jul	202	2 7/8	...	...
Disney	110	Feb	593	3	221	5/16
112 15/16	110	Mar	388	5 1/8	115	2
112 15/16	115	Mar	1185	2 1/2	5	4 1/2
DuPont	60	Feb	75	1	277	5/16
DuraPh	35	Mar	356	4	286	1 5/16
37 5/8	40	Mar	394	1 1/4	88	3 3/8
ETradeGr	25	Feb	30	1 1/2	520	5/8
EVI Inc	40	Feb	7	5 1/2	200	1/4
44 1/2	40	Mar	...	...	300	1 1/4
44 1/2	50	Feb	442	1/16	...	...
EKodak	65	Apr	211	4	43	1 15/16
ElPNGs	70	Jul	203	2 3/4	...	...
Elcom	7 1/2	Mar	300	1/2	...	...
EleArt	40	Feb	617	3/4	...	...
EnrgyGp	40	Feb	325	10 5/8	...	...
50 11/16	40	Mar	324	11	...	...
Enron	40	Apr	460	4 1/2	...	...
43 15/16	40	Jul	...	...	203	3/4
EricTel	40	Apr	342	4 5/8	405	1 1/8
43 5/16	45	Mar	425	1 5/16	127	3
43 5/16	45	Apr	251	2 3/8	12	3 1/2
Exxon	65	Mar	456	5/8	2	2 7/8
FPA Md	17 1/2	Aug	...	...	200	2 1/2
21 1/8	25	Aug	200	2 3/4	...	...
F N M	60	Feb	360	4 7/8	102	1/16
64 7/8	60	Jun	505	7 1/2	127	2
64 7/8	65	Mar	400	2 7/16	10	2 1/2
64 7/8	65	Jun	570	4 3/4	12	4 1/8
64 7/8	70	Mar	281	5/8	28	5 1/2
FfthThrd	80	Feb	210	3/4	...	...
FilaHold	30	Jul	235	1 3/16	...	...
FUnion	45	Apr	273	5 3/4	...	...
Firstar	40	Feb	200	1	...	...
FleetF	55	Apr	1740	24	...	...
78 9/16	65	Jul	1750	14 3/4	...	...
78 9/16	70	Apr	261	9 1/2	...	...
Fluor	45	Mar	222	1 3/8	5	2
43 7/8	45	Apr	243	1 15/16	60	2 3/4
Ford	40	Mar	300	14 1/4	...	...

Option/Strike		Exp.	Call Vol.	Call Last	Put Vol.	Put Last
66 3/4	65	Feb	286	2	11	3/16
66 3/4	65	Mar	1097	3 1/8	189	1 3/16
66 3/4	65	May	293	5	29	2 1/2
66 3/4	65	Aug	488	7	4	3 3/4
66 3/4	70	Mar	1656	1	33	4
66 3/4	70	Aug	382	4 3/8	...	...
HostMar	17 1/2	Jul	...	...	1000	1
17 7/8	20	Mar	300	3/8	...	...
HutchT	25	Aug	...	...	300	3 7/8
IDEC	45	Mar	312	2 3/4	320	3 3/4
ITT Cp n	80	Feb	8	4	300	3/8
83 11/16	80	Mar	441	5 5/8	...	...
83 11/16	85	Sep	200	7	...	...
IXC Com	50	Aug	232	6	...	...
[illegible]	10	Apr	[illegible]	[illegible]	...	...
7 3/4	10	Jul	734	1 1/16	...	...
Infrmx	5	May	257	3 1/2	6	1/4
8 1/8	7 1/2	Feb	1013	3/4	55	1/16
8 1/8	7 1/2	Mar	276	1 1/8	20	3/8
8 1/8	7 1/2	May	335	1 5/8	40	3/4
8 1/8	10	Mar	254	5/16	26	2
8 1/8	10	May	372	3/4	15	2 1/4
8 1/8	10	Aug	223	1 1/4	26	2 11/16
Innovex	22 1/2	Feb	226	2 1/8	...	...
24 17/32	25	Feb	66	9/16	290	13/16
IntgDv	15	Feb	321	1/8	14	3/8
[illegible]	[illegible]	Mar	[illegible]	[illegible]	2	[illegible]
14 11/16	17 1/2	May	1076	3/4	...	...
14 11/16	17 1/2	Aug	478	1 7/16	...	...
Intel	75	Feb	308	9 3/4	18	1/16
84 5/8	75	Mar	22	10	213	7/16
84 5/8	80	Feb	1206	4 3/4	278	1/8
84 5/8	80	Mar	715	6 1/2	407	1 1/4
84 5/8	85	Feb	3702	13/16	1617	1 1/8
84 5/8	85	Mar	904	2 7/8	515	3 1/8
84 5/8	85	Apr	562	4 3/4	283	4 1/8
84 5/8	85	Jul	33	7 5/8	516	6 7/8
84 5/8	90	Feb	1870	1/16	142	5 1/2
84 5/8	90	Mar	1074	1 3/16	68	6 1/8
84 5/8	90	Apr	533	2 1/2	106	7 1/2
84 5/8	90	Jul	200	5 5/8	24	9 1/4
84 5/8	95	Mar	349	3/8	4	10 1/4
84 5/8	95	Apr	157	1 1/4	200	11 1/2
84 5/8	100	Apr	221	11/16	...	...
84 5/8	105	Apr	465	1/4	...	...
IntelectC	7 1/2	Mar	205	5/8	...	...
IntelEl	5	Feb	208	3/4	...	...
IntrDig	5	Mar	300	1/4	...	...
I B M	90	Apr	12	15 1/4	388	1 1/8
101 13/16	90	Jul	...	...	839	2 11/16
101 13/16	95	Feb	194	7	565	1/16
101 13/16	95	Mar	162	8 1/4	990	1 3/16
101 13/16	100	Feb	3001	2 1/2	2477	7/16
101 13/16	100	Mar	1320	4 3/4	1954	2 9/16
101 13/16	100	Apr	133	6 1/2	227	3 7/8
101 13/16	105	Feb	4948	1/4	1051	3 1/4
101 13/16	105	Mar	1914	2 5/16	334	5 1/8
101 13/16	105	Apr	375	3 7/8	148	5 5/8
101 13/16	110	Feb	700	1/16	20	8 3/8
101 13/16	110	Mar	835	1 1/16	15	7 3/4
101 13/16	110	Apr	539	2 1/8	15	8
101 13/16	115	Apr	282	1 1/8	...	...
In Pap	40	Feb	350	8 1/2	...	...
48 1/2	45	Feb	405	3 1/4	38	1/8
IntpbGp	55	Apr	200	1 13/16	...	...
Iomega	7 1/2	May	526	2 7/16	30	1/2

Listed Options Quotations page from the Wall Street Journal

stock that you feel is definitely moving up. I'll discuss how to pick those stocks, which are most likely to go up, in a later chapter.

A much more conservative (translated safer) play would be to sell the March $7.50 puts. Note that this put is out-of-the-money. Consequently, we are less likely to be exercised, that is to have the stock put to us, unless the stock moves down almost $1! Think about that for a moment... If the stock goes up, you're profitable, and if the stock stays around $8.125, where it currently is, you're still profitable, and if the stock even moves down slightly, you're still profitable. But how much cash flow can you generate from such a safe play? Refer back to the *Wall Street Journal* to find the premium for the March $7.50 puts. Do you see $^3/_8$, or $.375? On 10 contracts, that's $375 before commissions. What would your rate of return be? Let's see, $375/$2,000 = 18.7% for the month! Not a bad deal for a really conservative play...

Now, I want you to put this book down and go out to buy your own copy of the *Wall Street Journal*. Go ahead, you probably needed a break anyway! When you return, look through your own copy to see what returns you can find. I want you to determine for yourself that there are truly some really great returns out there for the asking. Remember when calculating your rate of return, simply divide the premium you receive for selling the put by 20% (or whatever your broker requires) of the strike price.

GENERATING CASH WITH NAKED PUTS

When selling naked puts as a business, you need to have an idea of the potential for cash generation. Think about the leverage advantage of simply buying stock on margin. If you have $5,000 in your account, you can buy $10,000 worth of stock on margin. This is $10,000 in buying power. That means a 50% margin requirement results in two times leverage. What kind of leverage then does a 20% margin requirement have? That's right, five times! Just look at what that does to your cash flow when selling puts.

If you have $20,000 cash in your account, how many of these types of trades could you do? Assuming that we can find several different stocks, which have numbers similar to the Informix example above, you could create about 10 naked put positions, ($20,000/$2,000 cash required for each position). This could generate around $2,000 x 10 or $20,000 per month in additional cash flow!

As I have already mentioned, very real risks are associated with selling naked puts. In the Informix example above, your risk is the entire strike price, or $10,000 on 10 contracts. There is, however, a way to manage that risk.

Suppose Informix were to remain around say, $8 per share. We would almost certainly have the stock put to us at $10. Since we have already received the $2 premium for selling the put, our cost basis in the stock would be around $8. We could either sell the stock at the current price of $8 and close our position, moving on to other trades, or there is another possibility. We could simply hold the stock until it went back up a little and then sell the $10 call to turn the position into a covered call. That's okay if the stock stays the same, but what if the stock actually falls to, say, $7 per share?

MANAGE RISK BY EXTENDING THE PUT

An interesting approach to managing this risk is to simply extend the put out to the next month. That is, on the expiration date of the put we sold, say the third Friday in March, buy the puts back. You would only be paying for the intrinsic value of $3 because the put is now $3 in the money. There is no time value to pay for here because you are doing this on the put's expiration day! As soon as you buy back the March $10p, sell the April $10p. The premium should be around $3 ⅛. How did we arrive at that approximation? Remember that the premium will be equal to the value of the intrinsic value plus the time value. We know that the intrinsic value of any $10 put on a $7 stock is $3. The time value, all things being equal, should be approximately equal to what we originally sold the $10p for when it was out of the money early in February, or around ⅛. What is the net effect in your account? You buy the March $10p back for $3 and sell the April $10p for around $3 ⅛. This gives you a net credit of $.125, or $125 on 10 contracts!

Carefully consider what just happened. If you had been right in March, you would have made money. But you were wrong! By extending the March put out to April, you made money. How often could this work? Probably every month you happen to be wrong! If you're wrong in April, do it again for May. At some point in time, you're probably going to be right, that is the stock will close above the $10 strike price and the puts you sold will expire worthless, leaving you free to move on to another deal. If, on the other hand, the stock remains below the strike price of $10, you could eventually make enough money by extending out to the next month then at some point you can simply buy the current month's put back and be out of the deal and still have made a profit!

If you work hard and become proficient at selling puts, you can generate huge amounts of cash flow with relatively little money tied up. Further, you can do so with relatively little risk if you are prudent in managing that risk by extending out to the next month.

COMBINATION PLAYS

A great way to generate a larger cash flow is to combine two or more plays on the same stock move. This enables you to double your opportunity to make money with only one move of the underlying stock. Let me outline what I mean.

Suppose you find Actrade (ACRT), a stock that looks as if it is on its way up. One way to make money is to buy a call, let the stock move up, and then sell your call for a profit. In this case, the stock closed around $16 yesterday, so you might buy a long-term call, say the July $15c for around $4. Another possibility is to sell naked puts on the stock. In this case you might sell the March $17.50p for around $2 and then buy those puts back for a lower price when and if the stock moves up. Of course, you could always just let the puts expire worthless if you think the stock will continue to move up on the expiration day. If you feel confident about the stock going up, why not do both trades at one time? We have already discussed the basic rules involved for each individual trade. These basics still apply when we combine trades. Remember, a good rule of thumb is to buy long-term and sell short-term, regardless of whether the trades are done individually or together.

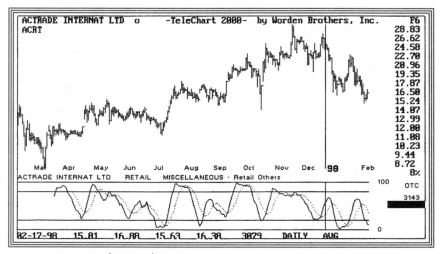

Actrade (ACRT) looks as if it is poised for a move up

What about when the stock is coming down in value? ACTL appears to be a likely candidate (see next page). It has peaked around $15, and started to move sideways. It looks like it is ready to move lower.

In this case you can buy puts and sell naked calls. Specifically, buy the May $15p and sell the March $15c. After the stock has moved down, sell your puts for a profit and buy your calls back at a lower price, thereby potentially doubling up on your profit!

In the stock market, whenever you begin talking about increased profits, you need to keep in mind that they are usually accompanied by higher risk. Combination plays are no exception. Since you are doubling your position in the stock, and your increased profit is predicated upon the stock's moving in a particular direction, you need to watch your position carefully. If the stock moves against you, that is, if it goes in the opposite direction, you stand to suffer increased losses on combination trades over individual trades.

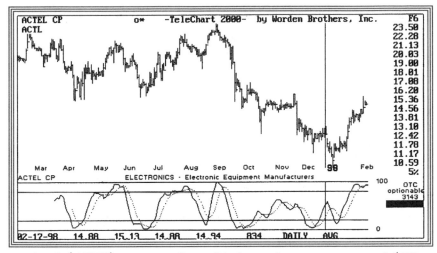

Actel (ACTL) seems to have hit its resistance at around $15

HIGH RETURN OPTION COMBINATIONS–SPREADS

Spreads can be a highly effective way to accomplish three objectives: generate immediate cash, reduce the amount of cash tied up in any one trade, and limit your downside risk. While there are many different types of spreads, I'll discuss just two here.

The first type is a "call debit spread." This is a trade wherein you find a stock, which is going up, and sell the call with a strike price just in-the-money. At the same time, you buy the call having the next lower strike price in the money. Simply stated, the object of this trade is to get called out on the call you sold, so you want the stock to continue to stay high. Let's try a specific example.

Suppose we are in October and Microsoft (MSFT) is trading around $132 and you believe the stock price will stay up around that level.

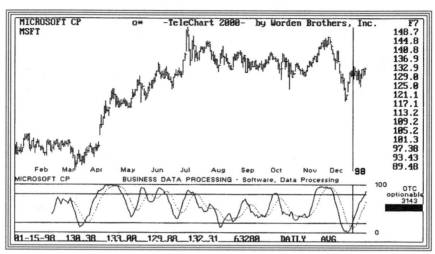

You think that Microsoft (MSFT) stock will stay around $132

You could sell the Oct $130c and buy the Oct $125c. Suppose further that the $130 calls sold for $8 per share and you had to buy the $125 calls for $11. This would create a "net debit," that is a net cost to you of $3 per share ($8 - $11 = -$3). On 10 contracts, that would be a net debit of $3,000. Why in the world would you ever make such a trade? If Microsoft stock remains above $130, on the 3rd Friday in October you will get called out on your $130 calls. That is, someone is going to buy the stock from you at $130. But you don't own the stock. You own something even better! You own the right to buy the stock at $125. On expiration day, when you are assigned, you will net a $5 per share profit from buying at $125 and selling at $130, for a total profit of $5,000 on your 10 contracts. Your cost going into the trade was $3,000, so your net profit was $2,000, not counting commissions. That nets out at a 66% return for the month. Two other things to consider here: what is your maximum risk and how much cash does the broker require to cover that risk?

First, your maximum risk is much less than if you sold naked calls. In such a play, your risk is almost unlimited. In this spread, the most you could lose is the difference between the price you paid for the $125 call, $11, and the premium you received for selling the $130 call, $8. That is a maximum potential loss of $3 per share or $3,000 on 10 contracts. When would you incur this loss? If and only if the stock price closed below the lowest strike price ($125). In that event, both calls would expire worthless and you would lose the maximum amount. If the stock closed somewhere between the two strike prices, say at $128, the $130 call you sold would expire worthless, and you would still own the in-the-money $125 call on the stock. You could then sell this call to recoup some of your original debit, or exercise the call and buy the stock at the discount price of $125. It is because of this that most brokers will only require you to have in your account an amount equal to your maximum loss potential, or $3,000 in this example. The spendable cash is generated when, hopefully, the stock closes above the highest strike price and this usually happens on the third Friday when you are assigned. So there are the three benefits to this type of trade: cash generation, limited risk, and limited cash tied up.

PUT SPREADS

A really interesting, as well as lucrative application of spreads is the "put credit spread." The same basic rules apply as previously discussed with call spreads. That is, you are still working with stock, which is on the way up. With this strategy, however, there are a few differences.

First, rather than buying and selling calls on the stock, you buy and sell puts. In the above example of Microsoft, you could sell the Oct $130p for say, $4 per share. At the same time, you could buy the Oct $125p for say, $1 per share. Notice that rather than creating a debit, your account is now credited $3 per share, or $3,000 ($4 - $1 = $3 x 1,000 = $3,000). That is, you receive your profit up front rather than having to wait until expiration day to have spendable cash. You can then take that $3,000 and work with it for the next month, thereby possibly further increasing your returns. Of course these premiums can vary considerably with market sentiment, as well as other factors, so each trade must be considered on its own merits.

I prefer put spreads for two major reasons. First, as previously mentioned, these are credit spreads, so you get your cash up front and can use that money to make additional trades. Second, if you are right and the stock stays high or even moves further up, the entire position simply expires worthless. There is no stock to buy and consequently, no commissions to pay! The amount of money the broker will require you to have in your account to trade put spreads will be based upon the maximum risk to which you are exposed in the deal, or the difference between the strike prices minus any money you take in. In our above Microsoft example, you sold the $130 puts and bought the $125 puts. If the stock goes down to below $125, you will be put the stock at $130. The broker can then use same-day substitution to exercise your $125 puts. That is, you have to buy the stock at $130, but you immediately sell it for $125. So the maximum risk in this trade is $5 per share, or $5,000 on 10 contracts. Of course, you have already received $3,000 in premium, so the maximum you are out here is $2,000.

SPREADS AS CASH GENERATORS

Consider for a moment how using spreads as inventory in your business can be used to generate cash. If we accept that the cash required for each deal is simply the difference between the strike prices times the number of contracts traded, the potential for profit becomes amazingly clear.

Since we have been dealing with $5 spreads and trading 10 contracts at a time, each deal requires $5,000 to create. If we can net only $1 from each deal, this means that each $5,000 we have to trade could generate around $1,000 in monthly income. Suppose you had $50,000 in your account. How much monthly income could you reasonably expect to produce? If we divide $50,000 by $5,000, we see that we can do 10 of these trades per month. If each trade produces $1,000 income, that amounts to a potential of $10,000 per month.

If you move down into stocks priced between $5 and $25, the strike prices are only $2.50 apart. Creating put spreads in this price range means you can do 20 of these deals. Using the same assumptions as above, we have the potential for our $50,000 to create around $15,000 per month in new income. I really hope you're starting to catch the vision of what is possible!

CHAPTER

9

FINDING THE GOOD ONES

There is in the market a field of study called technical analysis. This topic is the subject of several different college courses at the post graduate level and could consume the lion's share of most financial graduate degree programs. Obviously, I'm not going to go into that much detail here. It would hardly be appropriate considering the scope and purpose of this book. However, technical analysis is a very important tool for the serious trader, so I believe it deserves at least a certain amount of our attention.

TELECHART 2000™

To accomplish that end, we will be discussing various technical features to be found on stock charts provided by Worden Brothers, Inc. This company, world renowned for their expertise at technical analysis, offers a charting service which I use everyday. Their service is built around TeleChart 2000™, better known as TC-2000, which is a software package containing stock market charts for each of the stocks trading on a major exchange. On the next page is an example of a TC-2000 chart for Intel (INTC).

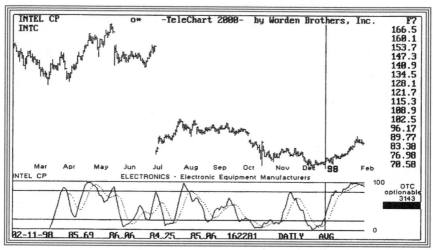

A TC-2000 chart for Intel (INTC)

Look carefully at the chart for Intel. In the top left corner is the name of the company. Just below the name is the appropriate ticker symbol. The numbers down the right-hand margin are stock prices. While the charts can be set up for different periods of time, this one shows the stock prices for the last twelve months. That means each vertical division across the chart is one month, with each month being labeled at the bottom of the price graph. Below the names of the months, the company's main business interest is listed. In this case, you read "ELECTRONICS - Electronic Equipment Manufacturers," a brief but sufficient description of what Intel does.

Below the numbers on the right side of the chart is printed the name of the exchange upon which the stock is listed, OTC for Intel. That is, of course, NASDAQ. Beneath will be shown the word "optionable" if the stock is, in fact, optionable. Along the bottom of the charts you will see a series of numbers. At the far left is the date of the chart. The next number "85.69" was the opening stock price for the day. "86.06" was the highest price attained by the stock that day. "84.25" was, as you may have guessed, the lowest price at which the stock traded, and "85.06" was the price at which the stock closed. The next number to the right, "162281," is ¹/₁₀₀th the number of shares traded today. So, by adding two zeros, we see that 162,281 + 00, or 16,228,100 shares traded today.

The squiggly lines just above these numbers are called "stochastics." That term simply means a comparison of moving price averages. The way I set up my charts, I look at the 7 and 9-day moving averages over a 14-day window. That means each day the moving averages are recomputed by adding today's values and dropping those values from 8 and 10 days ago, respectively. It is not really important that you understand what I just said but very important that you set up your charts so that they properly display these values. To do this, first bring up any stock chart. Complete instructions on how to do this can be found in the operator's manual. Once you have a chart up, press the "S" key. Enter the number 14 and another line will appear, allowing you to enter the second number, "7." After entering "7," enter the third number, "9." And finally, enter the last number, "2."

You have now set your TC-2000 up so that you have a short-term crystal ball with about 75 to 80% accuracy as to whether the stock will move up or down over the next few days or weeks. By the way, once you have entered these numbers, you never have to do it again unless you change them for some reason. We are now ready to learn to deal with simple technical analysis.

USING STOCHASTICS

Over the last two years of using these charts, I noticed that whenever the two stochastics lines crossed each other at the "bottom" of the chart, that is somewhere near the line labeled "0," then in about 75 to 80% of those cases, over the next few days, or weeks, the stock price began to move up. Look at the chart for INTS on the next page.

Start by looking at late April. Notice the stochastics crossing near the bottom? Now move up into the chart for the same time period. Within a few days, what happened to the price of the stock? That's right, it went up, significantly! Now move to late June when the stochastics crossed near the bottom. Look at what the stock did. It went up again. Look at September, December, and January. In each case, the stochastics crossing each other at the bottom was a precursor to the stock moving up. In only one case, look at October, did this not happen!

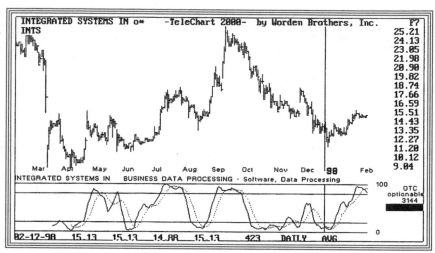

What happened when the stochastics crossed at the bottom?

Now let's look at what happens when the stochastics cross each other at the top of the chart.

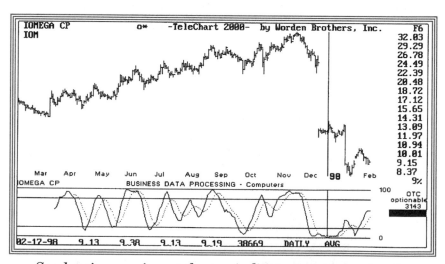

Stochastics crossing at the top indicate a coming price drop

Look at the chart for Iomega back in mid-April and notice that the stochastics crossed each other at the top of the chart. Now move directly up into the chart and see that the stock price began to move down until the last week in April. The same thing happened in mid June. Look at the first few days of December. The stochastics again accurately predicted a significant price slide.

Whenever the stochastics cross each other in the middle of the chart, I have found no consistent, predictable stock price movement. Sometimes the stock will move up, other times, it will move down. I've even seen it simply move sideways.

In order to keep things simple, I've devised a chart scoring system that involves only a plus (+), a minus (-) and a zero (0). If indications show a stock going up, I give it a score of plus (+). If indications show a stock going down, I'll assign a score of minus (-). If indications are not clearly showing anything, I'll give that a score of zero (0). If stochastics are crossing each other at the bottom, I'll score that as a plus (+). If they are at the top, I'll score that as a minus (-). If they are doing anything else, I'll score that a zero (0). In the charts we've just looked at, the stochastics on the Iomega chart score a zero because today they are neither crossing at the top nor the bottom. The chart for INTS will receive a minus on the stochastics because they are crossing at the top.

PRICE GRAPH

The next technical indicator to look at is the price graph. This is usually a jagged line running through the middle of the chart. This graph is really a combination of connected vertical and horizontal lines, which depict intra day trading highs and lows as well as the opening and closing values. While much more information can be gathered from this graph, we will concentrate only on the closing price, which is indicated by the short horizontal line for the day in question.

Since simpler is usually better, a simple approach to trading in the market might be to buy when a stock is low, and sell when it is high. We can use this pretty basic idea to score the price graph using a plus whenever the stock is on weakness, a minus whenever the stock is on strength, and a zero whenever the stock is neither particularly high nor low. But high and/or low compared to what? Let's use the 52-week high and low stock prices as our extremes. With your TC-2000 set on 52 weeks, the high and low values are very clear. In the chart for ION below, the 52-week high is around $45, while the 52-week low is around $33. In scoring the price graph for this stock chart, I would give it a minus (-), because the stock price is at its 52-week high value right now. Who wants to buy when the stock is high? By the way, how would you score the stochastics, and why?

The price graph shows opening, high, low, and closing values

I'd give the stochastics a minus because they are crossing each other at the top. So what is our chart score so far? Let's see, minus on stochastics, minus on price graph, that's two minuses, so far ...

MONEYSTREAM™ AND BALANCE OF POWER™

One of the reasons I use TC-2000 is that Worden Brother, Inc. has two technical tools, which no one else has—MoneyStream™ and Balance of Power™. To view these, simply press the letter "B" while you have a chart up.

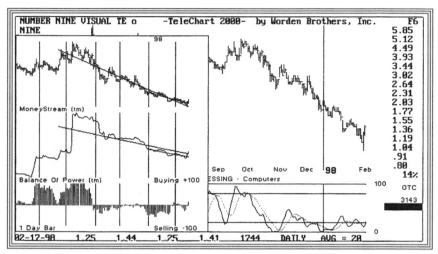

Pressing "B" will bring up the "Balance of Power Box"

You will see a box appear on the left side of the screen. This box will contain three charts. The top one you can ignore as you have already seen it. It is merely a duplication of the price graph, which we have already looked at. The middle chart is labeled MoneyStream™. I want to avoid turning this into a book on technical analysis, so I will explain this very simply. Consider the Moneystream™ to be an indication of whether new money is flowing into the stock or away from the stock. This might be considered a quasi-indicator of investor sentiment toward the stock. The chart consists of a yellow squiggly line and two straight, white lines, which are nothing more than long and short-term trend indicators. Ignore them.

Look at the squiggly line. If it is turned up on the end, that is indicative of new money flowing into the stock, a positive sign. Score this indication with a plus (+). If the MoneyStream™ has turned down, that is a sign that money is flowing out of the stock, a negative sign. Score that with a minus (-). If MoneyStream™ has turned flat and is just moving sideways, score it with a zero (0).

Look at the chart for NINE above. Notice that the MoneyStream™ has turned up over the last few trading days. Score that with a plus. How about the other scoring areas we've discussed? Stochastics are + and the price graph is +, giving us a three plus (+++) chart so far.

The last area to be scored is called the "Balance of Power™," or "BOP" for short. This is an indicator of stock accumulation. The chart is found at the bottom chart in the BOP box. It consists of a single horizontal axis with vertical lines above and below the horizontal axis. The lines above the axis are colored green and indicate periods of accumulation. The lines below the axis are colored red and indicate periods of sell off. If the vertical lines are very short, they may be colored yellow, which indicates periods of insignificant accumulation or sell off.

During periods of strong accumulation (green lines), the stock price is very likely to rise due to the supply/demand relationship. Conversely, during periods of strong selling, the price will most likely fall for the same reasons. For scoring purposes, if the BOP is showing accumulation (green lines above the axis) over the last day or longer, score that as a plus. If the BOP is showing sell off (red lines below the axis), then score that as a minus. If yellow lines above or below the axis are present, give that a score of zero.

Go back to the chart for NINE. How would you score the BOP? I see accumulation starting (one green bar above the axis following several red bars below the axis), so I would score this with a plus (+). What is our total chart score? Stochastics +, price graph +, MoneyStream + and BOP +. This is truly a four plus (++++) chart!

PULLING THE TRIGGER

So when would you use this information to pull the trigger, that is to actually do the deal? That really depends upon the trade you are considering. Suppose you are thinking about a covered call. Which way do you want your stock to move? Probably up, or at least sideways. What kind of chart indications would you be looking for to confirm that movement? Look for three or four-plus charts for your covered calls.

What about writing a naked put? Depends... If you are writing an in-the-money put, say you're selling a $15 put on a $13 stock, you definitely want the stock to move up, so only write naked in the money puts only on four-plus charts. On the other hand, if you are writing an out-of-the-money put, say you are selling a $10 put on a $11.75 stock, it's okay if the stock doesn't move up, so you can write naked, out-of-the-money puts on three-plus or higher charts.

You ought to get the picture by now. In any trade, the more the success of the trade depends upon the stock moving up, the higher the chart score you should demand. Of course, the opposite holds for trades wherein you expect the stock to go down. For example, if you are buying puts or selling calls, you want to do these trades on stocks whose charts have a score of three or four minus.

CHAPTER 10

STOCK SPLITS

One of the most exciting, as well as lucrative ways to make money in the stock market is to play stock splits. One reason I find them so attractive is that they are so predictable. It is precisely this predictability that makes stock splits such a simple strategy to implement. Another reason I like them so much is that you can make several different plays on the same company. In other words, you can play the same stock split announcement at several different times with a great chance to make money on each play!

HOW A STOCK SPLIT WORKS

When a company decides to split its stock, the company doesn't really decide anything. It is the board of directors who make the decision. If there are already enough authorized shares of stock then the board can have a meeting and announce to the world that the company's stock will be split. If there are not enough shares authorized, then the shareholders must vote on whether to authorize the additional shares necessary. The reason why the shareholders must vote on this is that the authorization of additional shares might have the effect of diluting the existing shares, that is making them worth less per share even after the split ratio is considered. For the most part, however, the vote is really a formality. I have never heard of shareholders turning down a split.

There are almost as many split ratios as there are numerical ratios. Arguably the most common ratio is 2:1, read "two for one." This means that one share will become two and each share will be worth half as much as it was prior to the split. So, if before the split you have say, 100 shares of stock and each share is valued at $50, then after the split, you would have 200 shares, each worth $25. Before the split, your holdings were worth $5,000, and after the split, your holdings will be worth $5,000. So you see, the action of splitting the stock doesn't make you any money, it's what happens after the split that makes this such an exciting way to trade.

Worth considering at this point is what happens to the options on each share in a stock split. When the stock splits, the options also split. That is, you will have twice as many contracts, but each contract will have a strike price, which is half as much as it was prior to the split, as long as we are still talking about a 2:1 split. Don't forget that the fact that you now have twice as many contracts has had the effect of cutting your cost basis on each contract in half. We'll talk more about options on stock splits later.

THE MORNING AFTER

The single fact that makes the stock split strategies work is that stock in a company, which splits its stock, is over 250% as likely to increase in value as a company who does not. I am not saying that if a company does not do stock splits, its stock won't go up in value. What I am saying is that viable companies who split their stock can see the value of that stock return to pre-split levels in a relatively short period of time, sometimes in a year or two, in more rare cases, in a few months! It is this pressure to return to its former value, which can make a stock split trade so profitable.

Let's go back to our $50 stock, which goes through a 2:1 split. Before the split, we had 100 shares. After the split, we have 200 shares worth $25 per share. Now let's say that stock goes up $1. Prior to the split, you have 100 shares going up $1, for an increase of $100. After the split, you have 200 shares going up $1, for an increase or $200 on the same price movement! That's twice the bang for your buck. Imagine what it would be on a 3:1, or a 4:1, or even a 5:1 split!

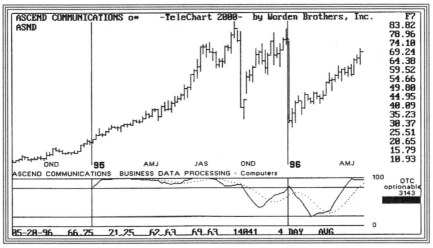

ASND split its stock twice within the same quarter!

Look at the chart for Ascend Communications (ASND). In October of 1996, the company split its stock from around $80 to around $40. Three months later, the stock was right back up to where it was before and split again, this time from around $75 to around $37.50. Suppose you had purchased 100 shares of stock in mid-1995 for around $40. Your total investment would have been worth around $4,000. Now, ride the stock through two splits, and sell it exactly one year later for around $70 and you would have around $28,000. The economic potential of stock splits is absolutely incredible!

DO YOU PLAY THE STOCK OR THE OPTIONS?

That's a really great question. The obvious advantage to trading the stock is that it never expires. Of course you do have to give up some leverage due to the higher cost per share for the stock. Go back to the ASND example. We originally purchased 100 shares of stock and had $4,000 tied up in the deal. When it was all said and done, we wound up with $28,000, a 7x multiplier on our money. Not bad...

But what if we had played the options rather than the stock? Suppose we could have spent that entire $4,000 on a May $40c. Paying around $4 per share for the option would have given us 10 contracts. After the first split, we would have 20 contracts. After the second split, we would have 40 contracts. Don't forget, that's 4,000 shares! Now sell those contracts in April of 1996 when the stock was at $60, a full month before expiration. At that time, the premium on those calls would have been around $50 per share. That trade would have netted us $20 per share x 4,000 shares, or around $200,000, a 50 x multiple!

Of course, it's easy to trade profitably using hindsight. And in reality, not many traders would have had the foresight to buy those ASND options a year out in the future. But if we know that stock splits exhibit a predictable behavior and we know what that behavior is in the vast majority of the cases, can we not turn hindsight into foresight with a pretty high degree of dependability? Of course we can. That's one of the reasons I play every stock split on every major company I can.

Let's talk about three specific times to get involved in a stock split and what the play might be in each case.

WHEN THE COMPANY ANNOUNCES THE SPLIT

When a company announces that they are going to have a stock split, the excitement and fervor is incredible. The stock will tend to run up rapidly! Here's a trade that I made just the other day on DELL.

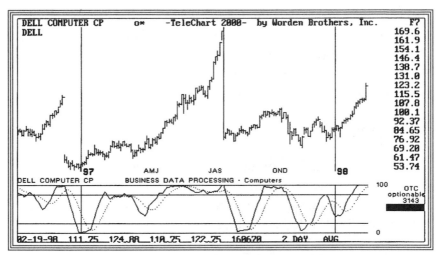

DELL announced a 2:1 stock split

Dell computers had been working its way up from the $80s and settled in around $111 per share. I bought a short-term call, specifically the Feb $110c around $4.12. The very next day, the company announced higher-than-expected earnings and a 2:1 stock split. The next day, the stock ran up to around $122. I sold my Feb $110c for around $12.06 per share, capturing around $8 per share profit. On 10 contracts, that's an $8,000 profit overnight!

While I purposely don't play every stock split announcement, I do play all of the announcements made by major companies, that is companies whose names and/or products I recognize. I rarely lose money on these deals if I do them right.

So, what is the right way? It's really quite simple. There are just a few things to keep in mind. First, make the play as soon as the announcement is made. If you wait to check company fundamentals, forget it, it's too late! I like to tell my students that you have about 12 seconds to pull the trigger. That's one of the reasons I use a stock market pager, so I can get the news as soon as it's announced. Second, the play is a short-term call. Do you remember what that means? (One to three months out on the expiration and an in-the-money strike price.) That's exactly what I did, played quickly (within 12 seconds) and used a short-term call.

Finally, know when to get out, that is, when to take your profit. If I had stayed in longer, I might have made a little more money, but there's really nothing wrong with putting $8,000 in your pocket overnight. In any of these plays, be ready to take your profit quickly, otherwise, you might lose it, which bring us to the second time to play a stock split.

POST ANNOUNCEMENT DIP

As we have already seen, on the announcement, the stock can run up very quickly. But very soon, the profit takers will move in and start selling. This drives the price of the stock down, and of course the option premiums will fall with the stock. Look at this chart for Microsoft.

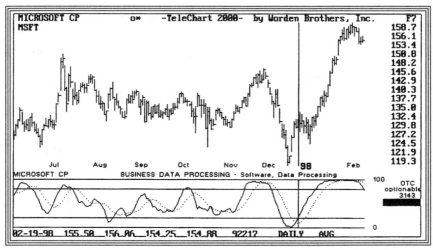

MSFT had an announcement runup but pulled back

Late in January, Microsoft announced a 2:1 split around $147. I bought the Feb $145c around $7.12. The stock ran up to around $150 and I sold my Feb $145c for around $9.50. The stock ran up some more to around $156 (see, I didn't try to take all of the profit possible), but then pulled back to around $154. As soon as it started to move up again, I bought the Mar $155c around $7.50 and sold them for around $9 when the stock moved back up around $157.

This is typical stock split behavior. On the announcement the stock will run up. But very soon, perhaps days, perhaps hours, the stock will begin to slide back down. When that starts to happen, watch it very closely. You are waiting for it to begin to go back up again. As soon as it starts moving, buy an in-the-money call with an expiration date that is one month past the split date. This is so predictable; you can make money on almost every one of these, if you do it right! By the way, buying one month past the split date is just my way of insuring that I have plenty of time left in the event that the stock does not behave the way I expect it to.

Is this really that predictable? Look at IBM's chart. Their last split was in May of 1997.

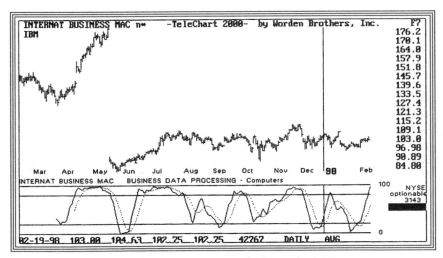

IBM split its stock in May of 1997

You can find the announcement by locating the "gap up" in late April. Now follow the stock price closely after the announcement. It ran up to around $157, then fell back to around $151. That's one dip we could have played, say buying the May $150c when the stock was around $152. Now look closely six days later. The stock rebounded to around $158 at which time we could have sold our May $150c. Then the stock began a run up to $176 five days later. When the stock began its run, we could have bought the May $155c and sold it four or five days later. That's twice we could have played the post-announcement dip. Including playing the announcement, that's three times to play this single stock split before it splits! Now let's take a look at what opportunities can exist on the day of the split.

SPLIT DAY PLAY

On the day the stock actually reflects the split, that is when a $50 stock starts trading at $25, watch carefully the movement on the stock at the market open. If it begins to go down, leave it alone. If the stock just sits there without much activity, leave it alone. If, however, the stock begins to rise, and this is important, at the market open, then get ready to do some trading! Look at these charts.

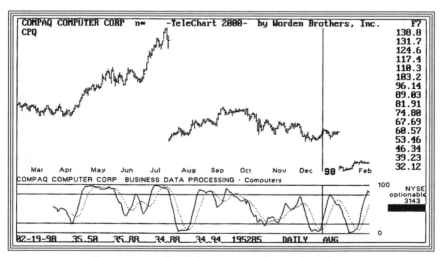

Compaq split then ran up for a few days

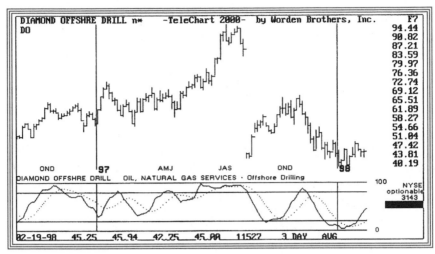

Diamond Offshore split then ran up for a few days

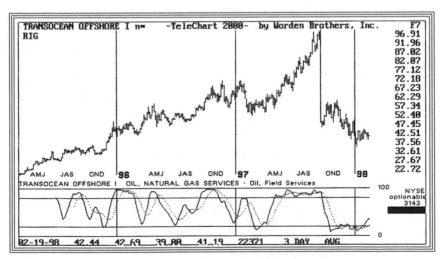

RIG demonstrated the same pattern

In each case above, on the day of the split, the stock started to move upward. It then continued upward for a period of four to eight days. This is typical behavior. If a stock split starts to move up on the split day, the play is to buy a short-term, in-the-money call when it begins to move. Sell the call as soon as you are profitable, but in no case hold it longer that four or five days.

Look at the chart for Diamond Offshore (DO). On the day of the split, you could have bought an August $40c and sold it four days later when the stock got up to around $50. Look at the chart for RIG. On the day of the split you could have bought the Oct $45c when the stock was around $47, and sold it three or four days later when the stock was around $51. Can you use these examples to determine for yourself what you should have done with the Compaq split? If you can't, give me a call and I'll tell you the correct answer.

We have talked about three different ways to play stock splits. The stock price behavior is very predictable. The plays are well defined and easy to understand. With study and practice, you should be able to look at the chart of a stock split company and understand exactly when and where to make the appropriate play. Remember the three different plays:

1. **On the Announcement**—buy a short-term, in-the-money call (don't forget that you only have 12 seconds before it's too late).
2. **Post Announcement Dip**—buy an in-the-money call, one month past the split date after the stock has pulled back and then started to go back up.
3. **Split Day Play**—at the market open on the day of the split, if the stock starts to move up, buy a short-term, in-the-money call. Sell when you are profitable or on the fourth or fifth day, whichever is first (don't be afraid to cut your losses here if you're wrong).

CHAPTER 11

MOVING TO THE BLUE CHIPS

As a child, I remember reading fairy tales about young men who left the security of their families to seek their fortunes. I never really understood what that meant exactly, but it sounded like it was full of fun and adventure. I even imagined that perhaps these intrepid young men might have to tilt at a windmill or two, or perhaps slay a dragon or conquer a giant before they would finally win that elusive pot of gold, which would provide for themselves and their families forever more.

In retrospect, I see more prose than poetry in how those stories relate to our real-life struggle to achieve some degree of financial independence. Unfortunately, most of us are well into our middle age before we find out that someone has neglected to tell us the complete story of how to seek our fortunes, how to accumulate wealth and preserve it so we can use it to provide for ourselves and our families later on in life.

What most of us are not told is that we need to be aggressively accumulating our wealth while we are young, energetic, and resilient. It is during our youth that we need to be building up our businesses, acquiring holdings, riding the financial bulls, and wrestling with the financial bears. Hopefully, by the time we reach middle age, our fortunes have been made, for the most part, and our attention and focus should turn to those strategies that preserve and maintain what we have worked so hard to acquire. These principles work together so that we may be able to enjoy the fruits of our labors when we reach our golden years.

All of this notwithstanding, I was 52 years old before I ever attended my first class on acquiring wealth in the stock market. What I learned both elated and frightened me. Of course I could make money in the market, I was told, but the bad news was that I should have started 30 years ago! Having a firm grasp on the obvious, I knew that I had some catching up to do. I was going to have to use some of the more aggressive (translated risky) plays to generate profits, which I could use to get myself back on the proper financial track.

All of the strategies we have discussed thus far have been very aggressive, and except for covered calls perhaps, very risky plays. These strategies are there as a *means* to an end, not an end in themselves. They should be used to raise the capital necessary to get our chronological age back in sync with our financial age. Strategies such as selling naked puts and creating spreads should only be used if we are playing financial catch-up ball. If we already have a large amount of assets, then we necessarily need to limit the amount of funds we choose to place at risk in such plays.

While it is almost impossible to quantify wealth or substantial assets, as a rule of thumb, I use the figure $100,000 as a benchmark. If you have this amount (or more), never, never place more than 10% of it at risk in the strategies we have been talking about. The other 90% should be placed into a carefully-thought-out portfolio of good blue chip stocks.

DEVELOP A BLUE CHIP MENTALITY

Do you think it is possible to put money into the market and, using only one, relatively safe, simple strategy, produce a monthly income which will allow you to walk away from you job right now? Is it possible that a fortunate few insiders have been doing this for years? Each year in my classes, I teach hundreds of students how to do exactly this using blue chip stocks. I'm going to let you in on the secret of how many of my students have been able to retire immediately after attending one of these classes.

An accepted standard of measure for the fiscal health of this nation's economy is the Dow Jones Industrial Average. For many years, this was the yardstick by which the stock market and subsequently the economy was gauged. A weighted average, the "Dow," as it is called, is a measure of the relative strength of thirty of this country's most highly regarded companies. These companies are commonly referred to as the blue chip stocks, and present us with an opportunity to generate a generous, relatively safe monthly income. To fully appreciate this, we must first understand who these companies are and what makes them safer than some other stocks. Do you know who the blue chips are? You should if you're going to make this your profession! Actually there is a list of them printed everyday in the *Wall Street Journal*. Simply look on the first page of the New York Stock Exchange Composite Transactions page, which is found very close to the front of the Money and Investing section. On the top left corner of the page, you will see a chart entitled "The Dow Jones Averages." Within that chart is an inset containing all 30 of the Dow Jones Industrial Stocks, the "Blue Chips."

When we discussed covered calls, you were told that to improve leverage, we should concentrate upon those stocks priced below $20. Increased leverage, however, is only one of the reasons we write calls on the less expensive stock. An equally important reason is that these stocks are more volatile. Simply stated, volatility is the tendency of a stock's price to change.

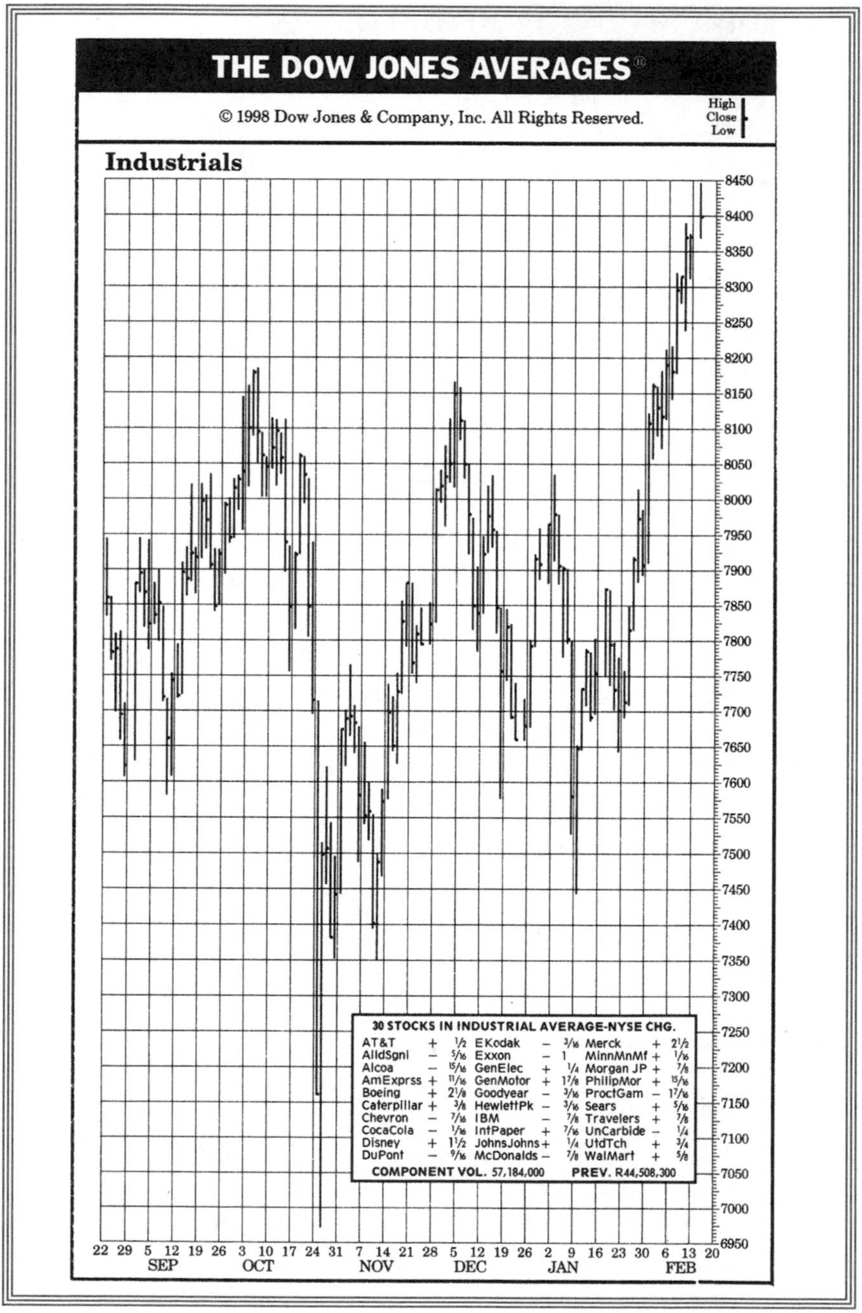
THE DOW JONES AVERAGES®
© 1998 Dow Jones & Company, Inc. All Rights Reserved.
High
Close
Low
Industrials
8450
8400
8350
8300
8250
8200
8150
8100
8050
8000
7950
7900
7850
7800
7750
7700
7650
7600
7550
7500
7450
7400
7350
7300
7250
7200
7150
7100
7050
7000
6950
30 STOCKS IN INDUSTRIAL AVERAGE-NYSE CHG.
AT&T + 1/2 EKodak – 3/16 Merck + 2 1/2
AlldSgnl – 5/16 Exxon – 1 MinnMnMf + 1/16
Alcoa – 15/16 GenElec + 1/4 Morgan JP + 7/8
AmExprss + 11/16 GenMotor + 1 7/8 PhilipMor + 15/16
Boeing + 2 1/8 Goodyear – 3/16 ProctGam – 1 7/16
Caterpillar + 3/8 HewlettPk – 3/16 Sears + 5/16
Chevron – 7/16 IBM – 7/8 Travelers + 7/8
CocaCola – 1/16 IntPaper + 7/16 UnCarbide – 1/4
Disney + 1 1/2 JohnsJohns + 1/4 UtdTch + 3/4
DuPont – 9/16 McDonalds – 7/8 WalMart + 5/8
COMPONENT VOL. 57,184,000 PREV. R44,508,300
22 29 5 12 19 26 3 10 17 24 31 7 14 21 28 5 12 19 26 2 9 16 23 30 6 13 20
SEP OCT NOV DEC JAN FEB

The Dow Jones Averages Chart listing the "Blue Chips"

High volatility, then, implies that the price changes would tend to be more frequent or more pronounced, or perhaps both. A less volatile stock would have a more stable price behavior. Volatile stocks, which are optionable, are of particular interest to us for option plays because the premiums on these options tend to be higher than those on the more stable stocks. This simply means that trading options on the more volatile stocks will generally result in larger profits (or losses). This is great given that you understand and, more importantly, are able to correctly manage that risk. One of my class students once asked, "Mr. Eldridge, risk is risk, so how can risk be managed?" His was a very astute question, which I really think most of the rest of the class missed, so I asked him, "Have you ever traded options?" His answer was no. "Well, if you have never traded options, who do you think has the higher level of risk in trading the same option, you or me?" I asked. "Of course, I do," came his response. "So class, isn't the risk associated with the trade really more a function of the trader than the trade?" I asked. "And if that is true, what is the only difference between me and you?" The response was an almost unanimous "Knowledge and experience!" I hope this important point is not lost on you. We manage risk by *learning* all we can about option movement on volatile stocks and then we *practice* trading them to gain the experience.

The converse of this is also true. That is, options on the less volatile stocks will have premiums that are lower, resulting in a lower margin of profit. However, the less volatile stocks are by definition less likely to be susceptible to wide or frequent price swings, so the stock prices are more predictable. In my home study tapes, I like to stress the point that this predictability is precisely what provides us with the margin of safety we like to see in our *less*-aggressive, longer-term trades.

This fact can be seen graphically by comparing on the same chart, stock price performance of blue chip stocks to the more highly volatile tech sector stocks. In the graph, we compare International Paper to Iomega. When playing options, Iomega will usually have much larger premiums than International Paper due mainly to higher lever of volatility of Iomega. This simply means that our larger, more impressive returns will generally come from less expensive and more volatile stock.

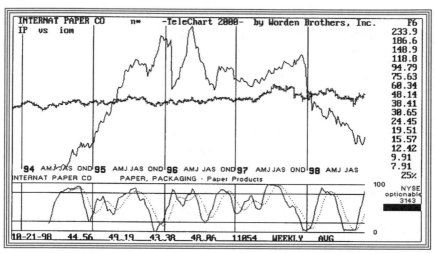

Blue Chip IP compared to tech stock IOM

Blue chip stocks are generally the more expensive stocks and demonstrate inherent price stability, barring dramatic news on the stock. Consequently as we move from the more risky trades to those with increased stability, we will generally be moving toward the blue chip companies. So how do you actually put together a good blue chip portfolio? Let me show you how my students quickly learn to trade with the big boys and girls.

Let's start with a list of the 30 Dow Jones Industrial stocks, or the Blue Chips.

1. AT&T (T)	16. Hewlett Packard (HWP)
2. Allied Signal (ALD)	17. IBM (IBM)
3. Alcoa (AA)	18. Int'l Paper (IP)
4. Am. Express (AXP)	19. Johnson & Johnson (JNJ)
5. Boeing (BA)	20. McDonald's (MCD)
6. Caterpillar (CAT)	21. Merck (MRK)
7. Chevron (CHV)	22. 3M (MMM)
8. Coca Cola (KO)	23. JPMorgan (JPM)
9. Disney (DIS)	24. Philip Morris (MO)
10. DuPont (DD)	25. Proctor & Gamble (PG)
11. Eastman Kodak (EK)	26. Sears (S)

12. Exxon (XON)
13. General Electric (GE)
14. General Motors (GM)
15. Goodyear (GT)
27. Travelers (TRV)
28. Union Carbide (UK)
29. United Tech. (UTX)
30. WalMart (WMT)

To begin with, blue chip stocks pay dividends. A dividend is a company's way of sharing the profits with its stockholders. When the company pays its dividend, each stockholder will receive a check for whatever amount he or she is entitled. This amount is, of course, based upon the number of shares the stockholder owns. From a current copy of the *Wall Street Journal,* we developed this list of all 30 of these stocks by looking at the inset of the Dow Jones Averages Chart. It is here. You can find the percentage yield of each stock's dividend. They are listed by stock in the sixth column, moving from left to right.

Quotations as of 5 p.m. Eastern Time
Tuesday, February 17, 1998

	52 Weeks Hi	Lo	Stock	Sym	Div	Yld %	PE	Vol 100s	Hi	Lo	Close	Net Chg
			-A-A-A-									
	48⅝	24¼	AAR	AIR	.48	1.0	29	458	47 9/16	46 13/16	47	+ 1/16
FD			AAR wi			...	...	5	31	31	31	...
▲	32½	17⅜	ABM Indus	ABM	.48f	1.5	27	126	32⅞	32 7/16	32⅞	+ ⅜
n	24 7/16	18¼	ABN AMRO	AAN	.25p	...	...	622	21¼	21	21⅛	+ 9/16
	11½	10	ACM Gvt Fd	ACG	.90a	7.9	...	603	11½	11⅜	11⅜	...
	8 7/16	7¼	ACM OppFd	AOF	.63	7.7	...	205	8¼	8⅛	8 3/16	+ 1/16
	10¼	8⅞	ACM SecFd	GSF	.90	8.9	...	1409	10 3/16	10⅛	10⅛	− 1/16
	7	6¼	ACM SpctmFd	SI	.57	8.4	...	749	6 13/16	6 11/16	6 13/16	+ 1/16
	15	12¼	ACM MgdDlr	ADF	1.35a	9.6	...	308	14⅛	14	14	− 1/16
	10 9/16	9⅜	ACM MgdInco	AMF	.90a	8.8	...	335	10 5/16	10 3/16	10¼	+ 1/16
	15⅛	12½	ACM MuniSec	AMU	.90	6.2	...	51	14 9/16	14½	14 9/16	+ 1/16
	27½	17⅝ ♣	ACX Tch A	ACX		...	24	131	24 5/16	23½	23½	− 11/16
s	49⅝	27½ ♣	AES Cp	AES		...	37	2336	41 13/16	40⅞	41¼	− ¼
x	61⅞	37½ ♣	AFLAC	AFL	.46	.8	15	1766	60 13/16	59⅞	60⅝	+ 13/16
	36 5/16	25	AGCO Cp	AG	.04	.1	11	3779	29½	28¾	29	+ 3/16
	21 5/16	17¾	AGL Res	ATG	1.08	5.2	16	1274	20 13/16	20¼	20 11/16	+ ⅜
	20¼	**13⅝**	**AgSvcAm**	**ASV**		**...**	**18**	**288**	**17 15/16**	**16 7/16**	**17 11/16**	**+ 1 3/16**
n	25 15/16	24⅝	AICI CanTr pf		2.25	8.7		16	25⅞	25 11/16	25⅞	+ ¼

The New York Stock Exchange Composite Transaction Page

Now, find and rank each of these stocks based upon the percentage dividend figure listed in the column headed "% Yld." Let me prepare you, this might take a couple of hours to do, but is worth the time. You will have to find each stock listed in alphabetical order. List the stocks from the highest paying dividend to the lowest. When I did this for myself, my list looked like this:

1.	MO	3.7 %	11.	GT	1.9%	21.	ALD	1.3%
2.	T	3.6%	12.	S	1.8%	22.	PG	1.3%
3.	GM	3.5%	13.	MRK	1.8%	23.	HWP	1.1%
4.	CHV	3.2%	14.	UK	1.6%	24.	BA	1.0%
5.	JPM	3.2%	15.	GE	1.6%	25.	TRV	1.0%
6.	XON	2.7%	16.	UTX	1.5%	26.	WMT	0.9%
7.	DD	2.3%	17.	CAT	1.5%	27.	IBM	0.9%
8.	MMM	2.2%	18.	JNJ	1.4%	28.	KO	0.8%
9.	EK	2.1%	19.	AXP	1.3%	29.	MCD	0.7%
10.	IP	2.0%	20.	AA	1.3%	30.	DIS	0.6%

Source: Wall Street Journal 6/12/97

Don't be surprised if your list looks a little different, as mine was done some time ago. Now, make a second list containing the 10 highest paying dividend stocks. This of course will simply be your stocks 1 thru 10 from the previous list. Mine looked like this:

1.	MO	3.7%	$42 3/4	6.	XON	2.7%	$61
2.	T	3.6%	$36 1/4	7.	DD	2.3%	$111 1/8
3.	GM	3.5%	$57 3/4	8.	MMM	2.2%	$94 5/8
4.	CHV	3.2%	$73 3/8	9.	EK	2.1%	$83 7/8
5.	JPM	3.2%	$111 1/2	10.	IP	2.0%	$49 3/4

In a third list, rank these stocks based solely upon the current price of the stock. You will have to call your broker to get this information. Rank them from the highest price to the lowest.

1.	JPM	$111 ½	6.	XON	$61
2.	DD	$111 ⅛	7.	GM	$67 ¾
3.	MMM	$94 ⅝	8.	IP	$49 ¾
4.	EK	$83 ⅞	9.	MO	$42 ¾
5.	CHV	$73 ⅜	10.	T	$36 ¼

Finally, choose the five cheapest of these stocks, listing them in descending order and throw the other more expensive stocks out. By now, you should have a list of the five cheapest, highest dividend paying stocks gathered from all of the blue chips. This was my final list of five:

1. XON $61
2. GM $57 ¾
3. IP $49 ¾
4. MO $42 ¾
5. T $36 ¼

We are now ready to build our portfolio. If you have the money, buy 1,000 shares of each stock. Otherwise, buy at least 100 shares of as many of the stocks as you can. For our purposes, I'm going to use 1,000 shares of each company. When I developed my list, the stocks I came up with were Exxon (XON), General Motors (GM), International Paper (IP), Phillip Morris (MO), and AT&T (T). Your list may be different, but for simplicity, I'll stay with my list and use pricing which is current as of this writing:

1. GM $69.875 per share   - 1,000 shares = $69,875
2. IP $56.50   per share   - 1,000 shares = $56,500
3. MO $40.69   per share   - 1,000 shares = $40,690
4. T $47.50   per share   - 1,000 shares = $47,500
5. XON $67.875 per share   - 1,000 shares = $67,875
      Total cost of the portfolio = $282,440

An interesting side note here is that when I first started this strategy, less than a year ago, my total portfolio cost was around $253,000. That means that the combined values of these stocks has risen significantly in less than a year! Keep that fact in mind for future reference.

You now own a portfolio that would be the envy of most stock brokers. But what do you do with it? I certainly don't like the staid buy-and-hold mentality so prevalent today. If you are going to be doing this as a business, can you afford to own stocks and just let them sit there? The only cash generated by holding stock is the dividends they pay. This particular portfolio will pay around $8,000 for the year. You can surely do better than an $8,000 return on almost $300,000!

Go back to a strategy you learned earlier in this book. That strategy is covered calls. Why not sell someone the right to buy your stock away from you at a profit? Remember the rules: sell the next month's call at the next higher strike price over what you paid for the stock. Let's look at the *spendable* cash that would generate. Remember, these quotes are current as of this writing.

1. **GM $69.875—sell next month's $70 call for $1.875 per share, or $1,875**
2. **IP $56.50—sell next month's $60 call for $.625 per share, or $625**
3. **MO $40.69—sell next month's $40 call for $1.94 per share, or $1,940** *(Note - if you get called out on this one at $40, you'll lose 69¢ per share or $690, so let's reduce the $1,940 to $1,250 to keep our figures as accurate as we can.)*
4. **T $47.50—sell next month's $50 call for $.75 per share, or $750**
5. **XON $67.875—sell next month's $70 call for $.875, or $875**

Before we go any further let's agree on some basic assumptions. Let's first agree that the premiums on these call will be exactly the same each month for the next year. They obviously won't be. Some months they will be higher, some lower. Do you remember that the current value of this portfolio is higher than it was when I put mine together? That means that some months you will actually get called out of your stock and will probably have some *extra profit* from selling the stock for more than it cost. Don't even count that in your estimates.

If we can assume that each month the premium on the stock will be about the same, then let's see how much cash our portfolio can generate over the next year.

1.	GM	12 x $1,875, or	$22,500
2.	IP	12 x $625, or	$7,500
3.	MO	12 x $1,250, or	$15,000
4.	T	12 x $750, or	$9,000
5.	XON	12 x $875, or	$10,500
		Total cash from covered call premium =	$64,500

Add to this the dividend income of $8,000, and you have an income of over $72,000 for the year! Better yet, do this on margin and you will have a staggering $144,000 of cash generated in a twelve-month period of time. Do you think you might be able to retire on this amount of income?

Typically, in a class of 80 to 100 students, I will have from 10 to 20 people who are able to put this strategy into effect *immediately*. That means they *never have to go to work* again unless they just want to! Again, I'm using actual quotes, which were current at this writing. Call your broker *now* to see how much cash your sample portfolio would generate. And don't be surprised if its more, much more!

But what about those of you who don't have this much cash to spend on expensive stocks? It is to *you* that the strategy sections of this book are dedicated. Use those strategies such as buying calls and puts, selling naked puts, and writing covered calls to generate profits, which you can then roll into a good blue chip portfolio. Those strategies are simply a means to this end, that end being developing a great blue chip portfolio!

CHAPTER 12

DOUBLE DOWN TO INCREASE YOUR PROFITS

Now that we have spent some time discussing the strategies, I want to briefly talk about something you might want to consider doing if and when the stock moves against you. The strategy is called "doubling down" and, like it sounds, involves buying more stock or options if the price falls. After all, if you liked it at $10, shouldn't you love it at $8? Well, perhaps, but there are a few things to consider.

The key to making money in the stock market is to buy low and sell high. As we watch various stock and option prices, it is easy to watch the prices rise to a peak as bargain hunters buy in and then settle back down as traders take their profits. Most, if not all, stocks behave in this way and this gives us the opportunity to collect profits on each of these moves. Let's look at some specific examples.

WHEN THE CHANNELING DAM BREAKS

Not long ago, I noticed that Just Toys (JUST) would trade around $1.25 per share and slowly (about every month) run up to around $2. I correctly reasoned that I could channel this stock between those two prices almost every month and make a pretty nice profit. I would buy the stock around $1.25 and place a GTC (Good Till Canceled) order to sell it at $2. When the stock would run up to $2, it would sell and I would walk away with a 75¢ profit. This is around a 60% return!

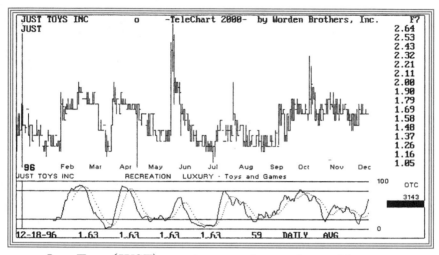

Just Toys (JUST) was in a consistent channel between
$1.25 and $2

The problem with channeling is that you never know if the stock will continue this pattern of behavior. Suppose you have traded a couple of these rolls and you buy back in at the support level of $1.25. How can you be sure that the stock will go up from here? Obviously, you can't! So what do you do if the stock starts down instead of up? To begin with, be very careful when you buy. Just because a stock has run down to its support level that does not mean that now is the best time to buy. It's certainly in the correct range, but wait until it hits its bottom (which may be below $1.25 in the JUST example), and then turns up.

LOOK FOR UPTURNS BEFORE YOU BUY

This is a good rule of thumb for any trading strategy. Too many traders try to guess at when to buy. They try to pick the exact tops for selling and the exact bottoms for buying. That is not only difficult, but risky. Besides, it is not necessary. Let the stock tell you when to buy!

For reasons we've already discussed, stocks move up and down for specific reasons, news on the company notwithstanding. In most instances, it boils down to either bargain hunting or profit taking. Once this activity begins, it should continue short-term. That is, the bargain hunters will continue to buy until the profit takers start selling. The profit takers will continue to sell until the bargain hunters jump back in. If it continues to fall, *wait*. Wait for it to turn back up before you get back in. Okay, but what if the stock falls below the support level, turns back up and then turns back down after you buy in? What do you do to recoup your investment? There are a couple of strategies here.

Let's continue the JUST example from above. You've channeled it a couple of times and you've bought back in at $1.25. Now the stock begins to drop below $1.25. First, you could sell the stock to stop the bleeding, that is, cut your losses. That obviously results in a loss.

A more interesting and possibly more profitable move would be to wait for the stock to find a new support level, let it turn up, and buy the same number of shares you bought at the higher price. That would give you a cost basis in the stock equal to the average of your two purchase prices, the higher price and the lower price. Now the stock would have to move up less than it would have before in order for you to be profitable. Sound confusing? Look at a specific example.

Using the JUST example from above, suppose you bought back in on 1,000 shares at $1.25 and the stock falls to 38¢ and then turns back up to 50¢. Notice here that the stock continued to fall and then turned back up. Your position is now down by 75¢ per share. On 1,000 shares, that amounts to a $750 unrealized loss. If you do nothing, the stock must rise $.75 in order for you to just break even. If you buy another 1,000 shares at 50¢, your average cost is $.875 per share on 2,000 shares. Now rather than having to move up 75¢, the stock has to move less than 38¢ before you are profitable.

CHANGING THE CHANNEL

Something else that might be happening is a change of range. Watch for the stock to start channeling again using the new low as a support level and, quite often, the old support level as the new resistance level. In our JUST example, the stock might start rolling between 50¢ and $1.25. Watch the stock very carefully here and be sure to check with your broker for any news on the company, which might account for the fall to 50¢ per share. If there is no news, be ready to take advantage of a possible shift in the channeling range. Notice that if you doubled down at 50¢, that is if you purchased another 1,000 shares at 50¢, your cost basis in the 2,000 shares is $.875 per share. If the stock channels up to $1.25, you have made around 38¢ per share profit even after the stock fell to 50¢ per share and never moved up past $1.25!

Doubling down can make money on almost any strategy and any stock price range. The underlying principle here is that most stocks channel. If you are dealing with a more expensive stock, you will probably be trading the options rather than the stock. For example, if the stock is channeling between $90 and $95 per share, it would cost too much to buy 1,000 shares at $90 and wait until the stock reaches $95 to sell. You'd be tying up $90,000 just to buy the stock!

In this case, when the stock is around $90, buy the $90 call for say, $5, then let the stock rise to $95 at which time you would sell your $90 call for around $8. That's a $3 return on a $5 investment, or 60%! Trading the stock would result in a $5 profit on a $90 investment, or a return of only 5 ½ %. Remember that the whole point of trading options is increased leverage, which generates higher returns on the same stock movement.

Using this same scenario, suppose you buy 10 of the $90 calls for around $5 and instead of going up, the stock retreats to around $85. You have $5,000 invested in your position. However, your $90 calls are now worth only say, $1.50, so your position in now worth only $1,500. The stock will have to rise considerably for your calls to be worth $5 again.

The premium would have to rise at least $3.50 to get you back to break-even. Let's see how to handle this situation.

PULLING THE TRIGGER

Any trade you make must have a triggering mechanism. There must be some circumstance or event, which tells you that now is the time to do the trade. The same is true for doubling down. Check with your broker for any significant news on the company. If you can find none, consider pulling the trigger. That is, buy 10 more of the $90 calls at $1.50. Your cost average is now $3.25 per share for 20 contracts, or $6,500 invested in the trade. Now how much would the stock have to rise before you are profitable? This is a little more difficult to calculate since option prices are not only a reflection of the stock price, but movement as well. Now the option market makers build belief and supply/demand values into the premium. That is, when the stock starts to fall, the call prices go down quickly. But when the stock starts to move back up, the call premiums return more slowly. In any case, the option premium will now have to rise by only $1.75 rather than $3.50 for you to get back to break-even. That may mean that the stock might have to rise as much as $3 or $4 to get back to that point. The key here is that by doubling down, you have significantly reduced the distance the premium and consequently the stock must move before you become profitable.

KEEP TIME ON YOUR SIDE

I want to make a subtle, yet important point about options. I hope you've already considered it. Go back to the difference between a short-term and a long-term option play. We defined a short-term option play as having one to three months before expiration. Long-term options have at least four months. An unstated assumption about doubling down is that you have enough time left on the option to allow your stock to move the distance and direction you want it to. If you only have one week left on the option when the stock retreats, you probably don't have enough time to justify buying more of the same option. The time value is eroding away so quickly that a huge jump in stock price (remember intrinsic value?) would be required to overcome that decay.

If you are short on time, you might be better off to simply cut your losses and promise yourself never to trade short-term options again! This simply reinforces the wisdom of always buying enough time whenever you trade options.

DISTANCE CAN MAKE A DIFFERENCE

The farther a stock or option falls, the more dramatic the effects of doubling down. I once bought 500 shares of stock in Autoimmune (AIMM), a drug company with a new product up for approval by the FDA.

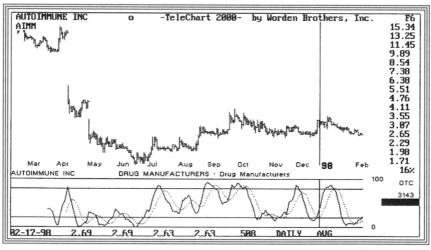

Autoimmune (AIMM) dropped dramatically to around $2

I paid $14 for the stock and within two weeks, the FDA disapproved the new drug, sending the stock plummeting to around $2. I considered doubling down. Purchasing an additional 500 shares at $2 would have brought my average cost per share down to around $8.

Before doubling down, AIMM stock would have had to move back up $12 for me to break even. After buying more stock, I was only $6 away from being profitable. What did I do? Remember that you should always do your homework before making any trading decision. I checked out the news on the stock and decided that the stock would probably be adversely affected for a long time. I decided that I would be better off to leave it alone and use my money for another trade. Look closely at the chart to see what AIMM has done since that time. Had I doubled down in this case, I would have tied up a lot more money for a long time in a potentially losing situation. What's the lesson to be learned here? Simply to do your homework. Don't double down unless you truly believe the stock has a chance of moving back up in a relatively short period of time.

Doubling down can be a fantastic way to take positive advantage of negative stock or option movement. Remember, however, to do your homework. Always run the numbers to see how much the stock would have to move to make you profitable again if you do the deal. Then decide if you think the stock has the potential to move that far and how long it might take to do it. These are both very subjective areas. Checking for any recent news on the company and historical stock price behavior can help you to make these decisions.

WORKING THE STOCK MARKET, SOME BASICS

I've included this short chapter on some basic principles of the stock market primarily for those of you who are really new to trading. For those of you in this category, it is important that you come to a full understanding of these principles before putting any money at risk. Some additional sources of stock market basics include *Learn to Earn,* by Peter Lynch and *Wall Street Money Machine,* by Wade Cook.

A GOOD STOCKBROKER IS CRUCIAL

In order to make money in the market, two things must happen. You must buy something and you must sell it! In order to make this happen, you must work through a stockbroker. There are basically two types of brokers, full service and discount. While there is a time and place for both types, I depend most heavily on full-service brokers. I depend upon them for two things, neither of which are advice. I want my brokers to give me service and information. The typical stockbroker's advice is to buy something and then hold it long term, realizing profits somewhere out in the future. In my business, I trade to generate cash, not long-term capital gains!

Think about it for a moment. If you owned a hardware store, would you purchase your inventory today and wait for the prices to go up before putting it on the shelf to sell? How long would you be in business with a plan like that? My inventory consists of shares of stock and various option contracts. I don't buy them unless I believe I can sell them quickly for a profit. The smaller the profit you demand, the more quickly you begin to generate that cash flow.

Finding a good broker, one who will work as hard at his business as you do at yours, can be challenging. But you must start somewhere, so start by asking around about brokers with various firms. Interview him or her as if they were applying for a job with your company. Here are a few things to look for.

1. Do they like working the market as much as you do? Ask if they are trading in their own personal accounts. A broker who is not a trader is more likely to cost you money than make you money.
2. Do they understand the strategies upon which you will be focusing? If you like covered calls, it is imperative that your broker be very familiar with how covered calls work, and how they don't work. It would be very helpful if your prospective broker used the same strategies you will be using.
3. Is there good chemistry between the two of you? This can help assure good communications and can help facilitate more profitable trades.
4. Are their commissions negotiable? Full-service commissions can be extremely high. If you are limiting your profit margin to produce faster cash flow, high commissions can seriously erode your profits. As a side note, don't be surprised if the broker agrees to lower his commission structure only after a few months of trading with you. Understand that he or she doesn't know you or your trading volume or abilities. They are much more likely to negotiate for very active, profitable traders!

CONCENTRATE UPON CASH GENERATION

This business, like any other, demands only three things for success: first, cash generation, second, cash generation and third, cash generation! One of the most significant reasons why new businesses fail is that they do not regularly generate enough cash to meet their monthly overhead requirements. To a certain extent, you can regulate your need for cash each month by keeping your expenses low. This is a great place to start, but you can never eliminate the need for regular cash infusions. You can never shrink your way to success!

The strategies, which I use personally and teach in this book, are designed to maximize your monthly cash generation while minimizing the amount of time your money is exposed to risk in the market. To better understand them, it is important that you understand the relationship between trading volume and profit margin.

Trading volume refers to the actual number of trades you do each day. Profit margin relates to the amount of profit you receive from each trade. Obviously it would be nice to receive the maximum return from each deal you do, but there is a trade-off of which you must be aware.

Consider automobile dealerships...

A Mercedes Benz dealer has a pretty high margin of profit built into each deal. The dealer has to because not many individuals can afford to buy the product. Consequently, while a large volume isn't sold, each deal returns enough profit to enable the business to survive. The Ford dealership across the street sells a large number of Escorts, but the profit margin is fairly small. Because of the large volume, the small profit received on each deal is sufficient, all other things being equal, to insure that the dealer can remain in business. Each dealership's service department operates on a similar principle. It is much more expensive to have your 500 SL tuned up than it is to have your Escort worked on. The main reason again is volume. You need to consider this relationship when managing your trading business.

I would much rather make a 50¢ to $1 profit on each of six different trades than to try for a $6 to $10 profit from one trade. There are a couple of reasons for this. First, the smaller profit is going to be much easier to get in most cases. Often, normal market fluctuations can yield these smaller profits, so you don't have to depend on some spectacular event to take place. Second, the smaller moves required to generate the smaller profit will almost always happen more quickly than the larger ones. This means that your money is at risk for a shorter period of time!

Another thing to consider is diversification. Never have all of your money tied up in one deal. Spread the risk out over several trades. A simple fact of life in the stock market is that you will not win on every deal, so don't expect to. A key to making money in the market is not winning on every deal, but rather winning on more than you lose!

It is important when beginning your trading business to decide upon how much cash you need to generate each month. I use a month as the basic unit of time here because most of us live in a monthly cash-flow situation. Our house payments come due monthly as do our car payments, utilities, et cetera. You need to be realistic when making this decision. If you presently spend $5,000 every month to meet your family's needs, then concentrate on generating $5,000 every month from your trading business. Don't make the mistake of thinking that you can somehow magically survive on less just because you're in business for yourself!

Now that you've determined how much cash you'll need each month, determine how many trades you'll have to do to generate that amount. For example, if you think you are capable of an average of, say, $500 profit from each trade, you'll have to make 10 successful trades each month. Of course, that determination might be hard to make until you've had a little more experience in trading.

Speaking of experience, how do you gain the experience necessary to consistently produce enough money to support your family without making the mistakes usually found within the learning curve of any new skill? Mistakes in the market are two-fold in nature. First, they *exist*. You will make them while you are learning to trade, everyone does. Second, they can be financially devastating. That is why *practice* is so important. There is a way to make these mistakes while you are learning in a way that won't hurt you financially.

That way is called paper trading. Paper trading is a way to practice a strategy until you get good at it. You simply find a potential trade which looks like it fits your strategy and pretend that you made the trade. Write it down just as if you actually did the deal. As mentioned earlier in the book, I've included some practice trading sheets in Appendix 1. Make copies of these sheets and use them as guides on each practice trade. Be sure to fill in every blank, as *all* of this information is important. Now comes the important part; follow the trade through until you can close the position out at a profit. That means that you will have to call your broker every day until you could have closed out on the deal. When your paper trading results in more profits than losses, you are ready to put your money where your broker is!

To summarize then, concentrate on generating small profits from large numbers of trades. Determine how much money you need to generate each month so that you can determine how many trades you need to complete and how much profit to try for. Finally, before putting any money in the market, paper trade your strategies until you show more profits than losses.

STOCK MARKET 101, SOME OF THE BASICS

Securities (stocks and options) are sold on exchanges. There are separate exchanges for stocks and options. Some of the more common stock exchanges include the New York, American, and the NASDAQ. The most familiar option exchange is the Chicago Board Options Exchange, or CBOE for short. Stocks are not sold on the options exchanges and options are not sold on the stock exchanges. In most instances, whenever you place an order with your broker to buy or sell stocks or options, you are not buying from or selling to your broker. He is simply placing your order with someone called a market maker.

It is this market maker who ensures that the stock market is one of the most fascinating places in the world to do business. Of course, there are some brokers or brokerage firms who are also market makers. In these cases, they are assuming two roles. A market maker is just what the name implies, a person or firm whose business it is to make a market in a particular security. In much the same way an automobile dealership operates, buying cars from the manufacturer at wholesale and reselling them to you at retail, a market maker maintains an inventory of a particular stock or option. He has purchased these securities from various sources at wholesale and remains prepared to sell them to you at retail. Various legislation passed over the years dictate that he must buy from or sell to you if he receives an order to do so. To insure the continuation of an orderly market, market makers use a quote system.

Each market maker posts a quote for the securities. This quote consists of two numbers, a bid and an ask. A quote is given in the form, "24 $\frac{1}{2}$ x 24 $\frac{3}{4}$." This is read as twenty-four and one half by twenty four and three quarters. These quotes are in points (dollars). In this example the bid is $24.50 while the ask is $24.75. This means that the market maker is willing to buy your security from you for $24.50 or will sell you the same security at $24.75. The difference of 25¢ is called the spread and represents his profit. Sometimes, if your broker is willing to shop for you, it is possible for you to buy or sell in the spread, that is at a price higher than $24.50 or lower than $24.75. This is an example of the type of service I expect from my full-service broker.

All trades are executed, or filled, from orders. There are two types of orders, market and limit orders. A market order is used when you want to buy or sell for whatever the current quote happens to be on that particular security. For example, if you were selling using the quote above, you would receive $24.50 for your security, assuming that the quote did not change before you were filled. If there was a change in the quote between the time you placed your market order and when it was filled, you would be filled at whatever the new bid happened to be. Be careful about placing market orders when quotes are changing rapidly!

A limit order can be helpful when the quotes are changing quickly. This type of order, to either buy or sell, contains a limit beyond which your order cannot be filled. For example, using the above quote, you might want to sell at say, $24 ⅝, which is above the current bid of $24 ½. You would instruct your broker to sell your security with a limit of $24 ⅝. If the bid ever moves up to your limit, you would be filled.

Limit orders can be further divided into either day orders, or Good Till Canceled, GTC. A day order is just what it sounds like. It is an order that, if not filled by the end of the day, is canceled. A GTC order is good until filled or until you call in and cancel it, whichever comes first. Most brokerage firms will not let GTC orders remain past three or four months. Check with your broker about his firm's policy here.

The last fundamental we'll discuss is margin. Margin is a term applied to what happens when the broker lends you money. Now this is not a loan in the traditional sense of the word. That is, you don't have to file a credit application with the broker. When you have invested all of the money in your account, the broker will stand ready to lend you an amount equal to what you've already spent on marginable stocks in order to purchase additional marginable stocks.

Exactly which stocks are marginable? The answer depends upon your broker who uses these stocks as collateral for your loan. It is therefore, up to the broker to determine just what stocks are marginable. For the most part, it is safe to say that most stocks priced under $5 per share are probably not marginable.

The major benefit to be derived from margin is that of doubling your rate of return. Let me explain. Suppose you want to write a covered call on a stock costing $5 per share. Let us further assume that you only have $5,000 with which to trade. With that amount of money, you can buy 1,000 shares of stock. From our earlier study of covered calls, we know that we can write, or sell, 10 contracts. If the calls are selling for say, $1 per share, we can expect 10 contracts x 100 shares per contract x $1 per share, or $1,000 to be deposited into our account on the next trading day. We have a $1,000 return on a $5,000 investment for a yield of $1,000/$5,000, or 20%. Not bad, but now do the trade on margin.

With $5,000, you can purchase 2,000 shares of stock. Your $5,000 pays for 1,000 shares and your broker will lend you another $5,000 with which to pay for the other 1,000 shares. This means that with $5,000, you have twice that amount, or $10,000 in buying power. Now that you own 2,000 shares of stock, you are able to sell 20 contracts, bringing in $2,000 in premium, rather than $1,000 as in the previous example. Recomputing the yield we get $2,000/$5,000 = 40%. The real point here is that you have made a second $1,000 using someone else's money!

In the example above, your equity, or ownership in the position is 50%. If the stock price begins to fall, your equity will fall also. If it ever falls to below 30 to 35%, your broker will ask you to send in more money so as to increase your equity. This is a margin call and can be bothersome only if you cannot send in the money. To prevent this from happening, never spend more than around 85% of your buying power. This will allow the stock price to slip without causing a margin call.

SECTION III

RESOURCES

APPENDIX

1

PRACTICE TRADE SHEETS

This Appendix contains the following practice trade sheets:

1. Channeling Stock Practice Trade Sheet

2. Covered Call Practice Trade Sheet

3. Selling Naked Put Practice Trade Sheet

4. Selling Naked Call Practice Trade Sheet

5. Call (Debit) Spread Practice Trade Sheet

6. Put (Credit) Spread Practice Trade Sheet

7. Stock Split Practice Trade Sheet

8. Blue Chip Practice Trade Sheet

CHANNELING STOCK PRACTICE TRADE SHEET

Date: ____/____/_____   Time: _____
Broker: _____

Company: _____   Ticker: _____

Trading range - Resistance: _____
Support: _____

FROM THE BROKER:
Current quote: _____   P/E ratio: _____

News: _____
_____

THE TRADE:
Shares Purchased: _____   Purchase Price:_____

GTC to sell at: _____

CLOSING THE POSITION:
Date shares sold: _____   Price: _____

Profit/Loss on this trade: _____

Notes/Comments: _____
_____
_____
_____
_____
_____

COVERED CALL PRACTICE TRADE SHEET

Date: _____/_____/_____   Time: _____

Broker: _____

Company: _____   Ticker: _____

Call to be sold: _____

FROM THE BROKER
Current Quotes
Stock: _____   Call: _____   Yield: _____%

P/E ratio: _____

News: _____
_____

ANALYSIS
Stochastics: _____   Price Graph: _____

MoneyStream™: _____   BOP™: _____

THE TRADE
Shares Purchased: _____   Purchase Price: _____

Call Sold: _____   Sales Price: _____

Associated GTC: _____

CLOSING THE POSITION:
Date shares sold: ____/____/_____   Price: _____

Call repurchased at: _____   Profit/Loss: _____

Calls sold again at: _____

Notes/Comments: _____
_____
_____
_____
_____

SELLING NAKED PUT PRACTICE TRADE SHEET

Date: _____/_____/_____   Time: _____
Broker: _____

Company: _____ Ticker: _____

Put to be sold: _____

FROM THE BROKER
Current Quotes
Stock: _____   Put: _____   Yield: _____%
P/E ratio: _____

News: _____
_____

ANALYSIS
Stochastics: _____   Price Graph: _____
MoneyStream™: _____   BOP™: _____

THE TRADE
Puts Sold: _____ Sales Price: _____
Associated GTC: _____

CLOSING THE POSITION
Date put expired worthless: ___/___/___ Profit/Loss: _____
Put repurchased at: _____ Profit/Loss: _____

Next Month's Puts sold(on a roll out) at: _____

Notes/Comments: _____
_____
_____

SELLING NAKED CALL PRACTICE TRADE SHEET

Date: ____/_____/_____   Time: _____
Broker: _____

Company: _____   Ticker: _____

Call to be sold: _____

FROM THE BROKER
Current Quotes
Stock: _____ Call: _____ Yield: _____%
P/E ratio: _____

News: _____
_____

ANALYSIS
Stochastics: _____   Price Graph:_____
MoneyStream™: _____   BOP™: _____

THE TRADE
Call Sold:_____   Sales Price: _____
Associated GTC: _____

CLOSING THE POSITION
Date call expired worthless: ___/___/___ Profit/Loss: _____
Call repurchased at: _____ Profit/Loss: _____

Notes/Comments: _____
_____
_____
_____

CALL (DEBIT) SPREAD PRACTICE TRADE SHEET

Date: _____/_____/_____   Time: _____
Broker: _____

Company:_____   Ticker: _____

Top leg to be sold (call #1): _____
Bottom leg to be purchased (call #2): _____

FROM THE BROKER
Current Quotes
Stock: _____   Call #1: _____   Call #2: _____
P/E ratio: _____

News: _____
_____

ANALYSIS
Stochastics: _____   Price Graph: _____
MoneyStream™: _____   BOP™: _____

THE TRADE
Call #1 Sold at: _____   Call #2 Purchased at: _____
Associated GTC: _____

CLOSING THE POSITION
Date called out: _____/_____/_____   Profit/Loss: _____
Call #1 repurchased at: _____   Profit/Loss: _____
Call #2 sold at: _____   Profit/Loss: _____

Notes/Comments: _____
_____
_____

PUT (CREDIT) SPREAD PRACTICE TRADE SHEET

Date: _____/_____/_____   Time: _____
Broker: _____

Company: _____   Ticker: _____

Top leg to be sold (put #1): _____
Bottom leg to be purchased (put #2): _____

FROM THE BROKER
Current Quotes
Stock: _____   Put #1: _____   Put #2: _____
P/E ratio: _____

News: _____
_____

ANALYSIS
Stochastics: _____   Price Graph: _____
MoneyStream™: _____   BOP™: _____

THE TRADE
Put #1 Sold at: _____   Put #2 Purchased at: _____
Associated GTC: _____

CLOSING THE POSITION
Date puts expired worthless: ___/___/___ Profit/Loss: _____
Put #1 repurchased at: _____ Profit/Loss: _____
Put #2 sold at: _____ Profit/Loss: _____

Notes/Comments: _____
_____
_____

STOCK SPLIT PRACTICE TRADE SHEET

Date: _____/_____/_____   Time: _____
Broker: _____

Company: _____ Ticker: _____
Split Date: _____/_____/_____

Strategy (circle one):
Announcement/Post Announcement Dip/Split Day Play
Call: _____

FROM THE BROKER
Current Quotes
Stock: _____   Call: _____

THE TRADE
Call purchased: _____ Price: _____
Associated GTC: _____

CLOSING THE POSITION
Date: _____/_____/_____ Calls sold: _____
Profit/Loss: _____

Notes/Comments: _____
_____
_____
_____
_____
_____
_____
_____
_____

BLUE CHIP PRACTICE TRADE SHEET

Date: _____/_____/_____   Time: _____
Broker: _____

FROM THE BROKER
Company #1: _____
Ticker: _____   Price: _____
Company #2: _____
Ticker: _____   Price: _____
Company #3: _____
Ticker: _____   Price: _____
Company #4: _____
Ticker: _____   Price: _____
Company #5: _____
Ticker: _____   Price: _____

Call #1: _____ Price: _____ x # of shares = _____
Call #2: _____ Price: _____ x # of shares = _____
Call #3: _____ Price: _____ x # of shares = _____
Call #4: _____ Price: _____ x # of shares = _____
Call #5: _____ Price: _____ x # of shares = _____

Total monthly premium: _____

Notes/Comments: _____
_____
_____
_____
_____
_____
_____

APPENDIX

2

STRATEGY OUTLINES

I'm including this section in the appendix so you can use it as a quick reference guide on how each strategy works. Please keep in mind that any two plays can be quite different even within the same strategy. What I've attempted to do here is to reduce each strategy to its most basic steps in an effort to help keep you organized, as you become familiar with trading in the market.

THE CHANNELING STOCK PLAY

I. The Strategy

A. By looking at the charts, find a stock between $1 and $10 with a sawtooth pattern, that is one which channels between two obvious values.

B. The next time the stock is at or near the lower, or support value, buy as many shares as you can afford.

C. As soon as your purchase has been confirmed, place a GTC order to sell the stock at the higher, or resistance value.

D. When the stock rises and you are filled on your order to sell at the resistance value, place another GTC, this time to buy the stock back down around the support value.

E. Repeat steps C, D and E as long as the stock moves between these two values.

II. Collecting Data

There's really not much data to be gathered on this play. Most of these companies are very small with market fundamentals that would make a strong man cower in fear! You're really playing the chart pattern more than anything else.

III. Analyze The Data

Again, you're mainly looking at the chart pattern. Not much to analyze, as the stock is either channeling or it isn't.

IV. Pull The Trigger

Place the order to buy the stock!

WRITING COVERED CALLS

To me, this is the Cadillac of the strategies. That is, there are faster ways to get there, but what a comfortable ride! Once you choose a good stock, there's nothing to do but wait until the call expires, or you get called out. In either case, you're automatically on to another play.

I. *The Strategy*

A. Find a stock between $5 and $20, which is going up slightly.

B. Buy at least 100 shares of the stock (It is usually better to buy 1,000 shares).

C. Sell the next month's call having the next higher strike price over the cost of the stock.

D. Wait until the 3rd Friday.

1. If the stock closes above the strike price, you will be "called out," that is your stock will be bought from you, so you are back to cash—go look for another deal!

2. If the stock doesn't go above the strike price, the call will expire worthless, so you can:
    a) Write the same call for the next month out, or
    b) Sell the stock and move on to another deal!

II. *Collecting Data*

A. Covered call candidate stock from *Wall Street Journal* or other sources

B. Yield of at least 8 to 10% per month

C. Call the broker to get

1. P/E—should be 20 or less for NYSE/AMEX stocks, or 40 or less for NASDAQ stocks

2. News on the company

3. Current quotes on the stock to be purchased and the call to be sold

III. Analyzing—Use TC-2000 Stock Charts

    A. Stochastics—crossing at the bottom, +

    B. Price graph—near the bottom of the chart, +

    C. MoneyStream™—turned up, +

    D. Balance of Power™—showing accumulation starting, +

IV. Make A Decision

    A. Do the deal

        1. Buy the stock and write the call at the same time

        2. On four-plus (++++) charts, buy the stock and wait for the stock to go up before writing the call, or...

    B. Don't do the deal

        Go look for something better!

SELLING NAKED PUTS

By far, this is my most favorite high-horsepower strategy. This play is really equivalent to writing a covered call. The major difference is that selling a naked put will often have returns that can be double or more the returns of covered calls. One really nice part of this relationship is that whatever candidates work for a covered call can also be used to sell naked puts, so you can begin to double up on your strategies.

I. *The Strategy*

A. Find a stock between $5 and $20, which is going up slightly.

B. On four-plus charts, sell the next month's put having the next higher strike price over the current price of the stock (in-the-money put).

C. On three-plus charts, sell the next month's put, having the strike price just under the current price of the stock (out-of-the-money put).

D. Let the stock price rise

   1. Buy the put back when you can net an acceptable profit, or
   2. Let the put expire worthless on the 3rd Friday

II. *Collecting Data*

A. Covered call candidate stock from *Wall Street Journal* or other sources

B. Yield of at least 25% per month (Remember on this play, yield = put premium/20% of the strike price)

C. Call the broker to get

   1. P/E—should be 20 or less for NYSE/AMEX stocks, or 40 or less for NASDAQ stocks
   2. News on the company
   3. Current quotes on the stock and the put to be sold

III. *Analyzing—Use TC-2000 Stock Charts*

    A. Stochastics—crossing at the bottom, +

    B. Price graph—near the bottom of the chart, +

    C. MoneyStream™—turned up, +

    D. Balance of Power™—showing accumulation starting, +

IV. *Make A Decision*

    A. Do the deal

        1. Sell the put having the first out of the money strike price

        2. On four-plus (++++) charts, sell the put having the first in-the-money strike price, or...

    B. Don't do the deal

        Go look for something better!

CREATING PUT (CREDIT) SPREADS

I really like this strategy for at least four reasons. First, it enables me to consistently earn returns of anywhere from 20% to around 40% each month on my money. Second, it has a built-in safety net, which places a cap on the amount of money you can lose in the deal. Third, it allows me to use candidates on which I've already done my homework, namely, covered call candidates, and finally, it allows me to move to a much better neighborhood of stocks if I so choose.

I. *The Strategy*

  A. Find a stock, which is going up slightly.

  B. On four-plus charts, sell the next month's put having the next higher strike price over the current price of the stock (in-the-money put). Also, buy the put having the next lower strike price.

  C. On three-plus charts, sell the next month's put having the strike price just under the current price of the stock (out-of-the-money put). Also, buy the put having the next lower strike price.

  D. Let the stock price rise and the puts will expire worthless on the 3rd Friday

II. *Collecting Data*

  A. Covered call candidate stock from *Wall Street Journal* or other sources

  B. Yield of at least 25% per month (Remember on this play, yield = net credit divided by the difference between the strike prices x the number of shares.)

  C. Call the broker to get

  1. P/E—should be 20 or less for NYSE/AMEX stocks, or 40 or less for NASDAQ stocks

  2. News on the company

  3. Current quotes on the stock and the puts to be sold and/or purchased

III. Analyzing—Use TC-2000 Stock Charts

    A. Stochastics—crossing at the bottom, +

    B. Price graph—near the bottom of the chart, +

    C. MoneyStream™—turned up, +

    D. Balance of Power™—showing accumulation starting, +

IV. Make A Decision

    A. Do the deal, or...

    B. Don't do the deal

       Go look for something better!

APPENDIX 3

AVAILABLE RESOURCES

Listed in this appendix are some of the resources available to help support you in your efforts to create and protect your personal wealth and financial security.

To order a copy of our current catalog, please write or call us at:

Wade Cook Seminars, Inc.
14675 Interurban Avenue South
Seattle, Washington 98168-4664
1-800-872-7411

Or, visit us on our websites at:

www.wadecook.com
www.lighthousebooks.com

Also, we would love to hear your comments on our products and services, as well as your testimonials on how these products have benefited you. We look forward to hearing from you.

SEMINARS AVAILABLE

S.O.A.R. (Supercharging Otherwise Average Returns)
Presented by Bob Eldridge

This one-day workshop begins by teaching you some basic trading strategies using a "hands-on" approach. You will be amazed at how easy it is to apply these strategies to the 30 Dow Jones Industrial Average stocks. Using these same strategies, Bob Eldridge, was able to resign from his job as an air traffic control specialist and begin speaking full-time after only a few months of trading!

The One-Minute Commute (Trading at Home)
Presented by Keven Hart

This one-day clinic will take you from being a semi-active investor to trading on a daily basis, giving you the freedom to dictate your own schedule and move forward on your own predetermined timeline. Trade from your home and stay close to your family. This condensed training will get you where you want to go by helping you practice trading as a business, showing you which resources produce wealth through crucial and timely information, selecting appropriate strategies, qualifying your trades and helping you time both entries and exits.

The Wall Street Workshop
Presented by Wade B. Cook and Team Wall Street

The Wall Street Workshop teaches you how to make incredible money in all markets. It teaches you the tried-and-true strategies that have made hundreds of people wealthy.

The Next Step Workshop
Presented by Wade B. Cook and Team Wall Street

An advanced Wall Street Workshop designed to help those ready to take their trading to the next level and treat it as a business. This seminar is open only to graduates of the Wall Street Workshop.

Executive Retreat
Presented by Berry, Childers & Associates

Created especially for the individuals already owning or planning to establish Nevada Corporations, the Executive Retreat is a unique opportunity for corporate executives to participate in workshops geared toward streamlining operations and maximizing efficiency and impact.

Wealth Institute
Presented by Berry, Childers & Associates

This three-day workshop defines the art of asset protection and entity planning. During these three days we will discuss, in depth and detail, the six domestic entities that will protect you from lawsuits, taxes, or other financial losses, and help you retire rich.

Real Estate Workshop
Presented by Wade B. Cook and Team Main Street

The Real Estate Workshop teaches you how to build perpetual income for life, without going to work. Some of the topics include buying and selling paper, finding discounted properties, generating long-term monthly cash flow, and controlling properties without owning them.

Business Entity Skills Training (BEST)
Presented by Wade B. Cook and Team Wall Street

Learn about the five powerful entities you can use to protect your wealth and your family. Learn the secrets of asset protection, eliminate your fear of litigation, and minimize your taxes.

AUDIOCASSETTES

13 Fantastic Income Formulas-A free cassette
By Wade B. Cook

Learn the 13 cash flow formulas taught in the Wall Street Workshop. Learn to double some of your money in 2½ to 4 months.

Zero To Zillions
By Wade B. Cook

This is a powerful audio workshop on Wall Street—understanding the stock market game, playing it successfully, and retiring rich. Learn powerful investment strategies to avoid pitfalls and losses, catch Day-trippers, Bottom fish, write Covered Calls, the possibility to double some of your money in one week on options on stock split companies, and so much more. Wade "Meter Drop" Cook will teach you how he makes fantastic annual returns in your account.

Power Of Nevada Corporations—A free cassette
By Wade B. Cook

Nevada Corporations have secrecy, privacy, minimal taxes, no reciprocity with the IRS, and protection for shareholders, officers, and directors. This is a powerful seminar.

Income Streams—A free cassette
By Wade B. Cook

Learn to buy and sell real estate the Wade Cook way. This informative cassette will instruct you in building and operating your own real estate money machine.

Money Machine I & II
By Wade B. Cook

Learn the benefits of buying, and more importantly, selling real estate. Now the system for creating and maintaining a real estate money machine is available in audiocassette form. Money Machine I & II teach the step-by-step cash-flow formulas that made Wade Cook, and thousands like him, millions of dollars.

Money Mysteries of the Millionaires—A free cassette
By Wade B. Cook

How to make money and keep it. This fantastic seminar shows you how to use Nevada Corporations, Living Trusts, Pension Plans, Charitable Remainder Trusts, and Family Limited Partnerships to protect your assets.

Unlimited Wealth Audio Set
By Wade B. Cook

Unlimited Wealth is the "University of Money-Making Ideas" home study course that helps you improve your money's personality. The heart and soul of this seminar is to make more money, pay fewer taxes, and keep more for your retirement and family. This cassette series contains the great ideas from *Wealth 101* on tape, so you can listen to them whenever you want.

Retirement Prosperity
By Wade B. Cook

Take that IRA money now sitting idle and invest it in ways that generate you bigger, better, and quicker returns. This four audiotape set walks you through a system of using a self-directed IRA to create phenomenal profits, virtually tax free! This is one of the most complete systems for IRA investing ever created.

The Financial Fortress Home Study Course
By Wade B. Cook

This eight-part series is the last word in entity structuring. It goes far beyond mere financial planning or estate planning. It helps you structure your business and your affairs so that you can avoid the majority of taxes, retire rich, escape lawsuits, bequeath your assets to your heirs without government interference, and, in short, bomb proof your entire estate. There are six audio cassette seminars on tape, an entity structuring video, and a full kit of documents.

BOOKS

Wall Street Money Machine
By Wade B. Cook

Appearing on the *New York Times* Business Best Sellers list for over one year, **Wall Street Money Machine** contains the best strategies for wealth enhancement and cash flow creation you'll find anywhere. Throughout this book, Wade Cook describes many of his favorite strategies for generating cash flow through the stock market: Rolling Stock, Proxy Investing, Covered Calls, and many more. It's a great introduction for creating wealth using the Wade Cook formulas.

Stock Market Miracles
By Wade B. Cook

The anxiously-awaited partner to **Wall Street Money Machine**, this book is proven to be just as invaluable. **Stock Market Miracles** improves on some of the strategies from **Wall Street Money Machine**, as well as introducing new and valuable twists on our old favorites. This is a must read for anyone interested in making serious money in the stock market.

Bear Market Baloney
By Wade B. Cook

A more timely book couldn't be possible. Wade's predictions came true while the book was at press! Don't miss this insightful look into what makes bull and bear markets and how to make exponential returns in any market.

Real Estate Money Machine
By Wade B. Cook

Wade's first best-selling book reveals his secrets—the system he earned his first million from. This book teaches you how to make money regardless of the state of the economy. Wade's innovative concepts for investing not only avoids high interest rates, but avoids banks altogether.

How To Pick Up Foreclosures
By Wade B. Cook

Do you want to become an expert money maker in real estate? This book will show you how to buy real estate at 60¢ on the dollar or less. You'll learn to find the house before the auction and purchase it with no bank financing—the easy way to millions in real estate. The market for foreclosures is a tremendous place to learn and prosper. *How To Pick Up Foreclosures* takes Wade's methods from *Real Estate Money Machine* and supercharges them by applying the fantastic principles to already-discounted properties.

Owner Financing
By Wade B. Cook

This is a short, but invaluable booklet you can give to sellers who hesitate to sell you their property using the owner financing method. Let this booklet convince both you and them. The special report, "Why Sellers Should Take Monthly Payments," is included for free!

Real Estate For Real People
By Wade B. Cook

A priceless, comprehensive overview of real estate investing, this book teaches you how to buy the right property for the right price, at the right time. Wade Cook explains all of the strategies you'll need, and gives you 20 reasons why you should start investing in real estate today. Learn how to retire rich with real estate, and have fun doing it.

101 Ways To Buy Real Estate Without Cash
By Wade B. Cook

Wade Cook has personally achieved success after success in real estate. *101 Ways To Buy Real Estate Without Cash* fills the gap left by other authors who have given all the ingredients but not the whole recipe for real estate investing. This is the book for the investor who wants innovative and practical methods for buying real estate with little or no money down.

Blueprints for Success, Volume 1
Contributors: Wade Cook, Debbie Losse, Joel Black, Dan Wagner, Tim Semingson, Rich Simmons, Greg Witt, JJ Childers, Keven Hart, Dave Wagner and Steve Wirrick

Blueprints for Success, Volume 1 is a compilation of chapters on building your wealth through your business and making your business function successfully. The chapters cover: education and information gathering, choosing the best business for you from all the different types of business, and a variety of other skills necessary for becoming successful. Your business can't afford to miss out on these powerful insights!

Brilliant Deductions
By Wade B. Cook

Do you want to make the most of the money you earn? Do you want to have solid tax havens and ways to reduce the taxes you pay? This book is for you! Learn how to get rich in spite of the updated 1997 tax laws. See new tax credits, year-end maneuvers, and methods for transferring and controlling your entities. Learn to structure yourself and your family for tax savings and liability protection. Available in bookstores, or call our toll free number: 1-800-872-7411.

Wealth 101
By Wade B. Cook

This incredible book brings you 101 strategies for wealth creation and protection that you can't afford to miss. Front to back, it is packed full of tips and tricks to supercharge your financial health. If you need to generate more cash flow, this book shows you how through several various avenues. If you are already wealthy, this is the book that will show you strategy upon strategy for decreasing your tax liability and increasing your peace of mind through liability protection.

VIDEOS

Clear And Present Profits
By Wade B. Cook

Wade Cook's 90-minute introduction to the basics of his Wall Street formulas and strategies. In this presentation designed especially for video, Wade explains the meter drop philosophy, Rolling Stock, basics of Proxy Investing, and writing Covered Calls. Perfect for anyone looking for a little basic information.

The Wall Street Workshop Video Series
By Wade B. Cook

If you can't make it to the Wall Street Workshop soon, get a head start with these videos. Ten albums containing 11 hours of intense instruction on Rolling Stock, options on stock split companies, writing Covered Calls, and other tested and proven strategies designed to help you increase the value of your investments. By learning, reviewing, and implementing the strategies taught here, you will gain the knowledge and the confidence to take control of your investments, and get your money to work hard for you.

The Next Step Video Series
By Team Wall Street

The advanced version of the Wall Street Workshop. Full of power-packed strategies from Wade Cook, this is not a duplicate of the Wall Street Workshop, but a very important partner. The methods taught in this seminar will supercharge the strategies taught in the Wall Street Workshop and teach you even more ways to make more money!

In The Next Step, you'll learn how to find the stocks to fit formulas using technical analysis, fundamentals, home trading tools, and more.

Build Perpetual Income (BPI)-A videocassette
By Wade B. Cook

Wade Cook Seminars, Inc. is proud to present Build Perpetual Income, the latest in our ever-expanding series of seminar home study courses. In this video, you will learn powerful real estate cash-flow generating techniques, such as:

- Power negotiating strategies
- Buying and selling mortgages
- Writing contracts
- Finding and buying discount properties
- Avoiding debt

ASSORTED RESOURCES

Wealth Information Network™ (WIN™)

This subscription Internet service provides you with the latest financial formulas and updated entity structuring strategies. New, timely information is entered Monday through Friday, sometimes four or five times a day. Wade Cook and his Team Wall Street staff write for WIN, giving you updates on their own current stock plays, companies who announced earnings, companies who announced stock splits, and the latest trends in the market.

WIN is also divided into categories according to specific strategies and contains archives of all our trades so you can view our history. If you are just getting started in the stock market, this is a great way to follow people who are experiencing above-average returns. If you are experienced already, it's the way to confirm your feelings and research with others who are generating wealth through the stock market.

IQ Pager™

This is a system that beeps you as events and announcements are made on Wall Street. With IQ Pager, you'll receive information about events like major stock split announcements, earnings surprises, important mergers and acquisitions, judgments or court decisions involving big companies, important bankruptcy announcements, big winners and losers, and disasters. If you're getting your financial information from the evening news, you're getting it too late. The key to the stock market is timing. Especially when you're trading in options, you need up-to-the-minute (or second) information. You cannot afford to sit at a computer all day looking for news or wait for your broker to call. IQ Pager is the ideal partner to the Wealth Information Network (WIN).

The Incorporation Handbook
By Wade B. Cook

Incorporation made easy! This handbook tells you who, why, and, most importantly, how to incorporate. Included are samples of the forms you will use when you incorporate, as well as a step-by-step guide from the experts.

ABOUT THE AUTHOR

Bob Eldridge is a native of San Jose, California. As a child, he was reared in Texas, graduating from high school in Odessa, Texas. He served with the United States Air Force from 1964 until 1968, completing two tours of  duty in Southeast Asia during the Vietnamese War. He graduated from Stephen F. Austin State University in Nacogdoches, Texas in 1971 with a B.S. Degree in Mathematics, Education and History. He finished his M.S. degree in 1975, majoring in Mathematics Education.

Bob taught mathematics from 1971 until 1976 when he became an air traffic control specialist with the Federal Aviation Administration. From 1979 until 1981, Bob served as an instructor for the FAA at the Mike Moroney Aeronautical Center in Oklahoma City, Oklahoma.

A commercially licensed pilot, he has been actively involved in aviation since his Air Force days, and is a past chapter president of the Experimental Aircraft Association. Still an active member of the EAA, Bob has completed three experimental aircraft projects. In addition to owning and flying an experimental Glasair aircraft, Bob flies a Beechcraft Baron to and from many of his speaking engagements.

He left the FAA in 1995 to begin a career as a personal stock and options trader and his successes in the market have placed him in high demand as a teacher and lecturer.

Bob married Miss Barbara Oxford of Ft. Worth, Texas in 1971 and they have two sons, David Allan, 17, and Christopher Thomas, 14. The family resides in Jonesboro, Arkansas and all are active members of the Church of Jesus Christ of Latter-day Saints.